Stretch You Wings

Wings

Famous **Black**
Quotations
For Teens

Selected and
Edited by
Janet Cheatham Bell
and
Lucille Usher Freeman

Little, Brown and Company
BOSTON NEW YORK LONDON

For America's Promise — The Alliance for Youth

Other titles by Janet Cheatham Bell

Famous Black Quotations
Victory of the Spirit: Meditations on Black Quotations
The Soul of Success: Inspiring Quotations for Entrepreneurs

First Edition

Copyright acknowledgments appear on page 166.

Library of Congress Cataloging-in-Publication Data

Stretch your wings : famous black quotations for teens / selected and edited by Janet Cheatham Bell and Lucille Usher Freeman.
    p. cm.
    Includes index.
    Summary: A collection of black quotations and African proverbs, arranged in such categories as: Knowing Who I Am, Family: Joy or Nightmare, Making Better Choices, What about Racism, and Hold Fast to Dreams.
    ISBN 0-316-03825-3
    1. Afro-Americans Quotations Juvenile literature. 2. Quotations, American — Afro-American authors Juvenile literature. [1. Afro-Americans Quotations. 2. Quotations.] I. Bell, Janet Cheatham. II. Freeman, Lucille Usher.
PN6081.3.S77 1999
973'.0496073'00922—dc21   99-13045

10 9 8 7 6 5 4 3 2 1

MV-NY

Printed in the United States of America

You're eagles! Stretch your wings and fly to the sky!

—**Ronald McNair,** astronaut

Ronald McNair was born in 1950 in South Carolina, where he attended segregated public schools. In addition to being valedictorian of his high school class, he was a leader in track and football. McNair graduated from North Carolina A&T State University, a historically black college, with a B.S. degree in physics. In 1977 he earned a Ph.D. in quantum electronics and laser technology from the Massachusetts Institute of Technology, Cambridge. He was chosen as one of the first three African Americans to enter the astronaut training program in January 1978 and became the second black to fly in space in 1984. McNair was a mission specialist aboard the spaceship Challenger that exploded in flight in 1986.

CONTENTS

PREFACE

When the laughter and flirtatious moments had ceased, the presenter asked the teens, who had gathered in the conference room, what they would do or become if no limits whatsoever were placed on them. He encouraged them to dream big, then to dream even bigger. Next, he passed out sheets of paper and asked them to write down all the things that could possibly prevent them from achieving their highest aspirations and dreams.

After a few minutes, he instructed the group to imitate him. The presenter took his sheet of paper and in deliberate motions balled it up, crumpling it in his hands, then threw it forcefully over his shoulder. Pleasure and surprise filled the faces of the teens as they imitated the presenter and ball after crumpled ball of paper flew over shoulders and landed on the floor.

When things settled down, the presenter emphatically said, "Nothing can stand between you and your dreams. *You* have the power to crush the obstacles. They cannot crush you."

Often we look at those who have achieved respect, admiration, fame, and success, and tell ourselves that we can't be like them because they've not had the problems we have. We believe talent, money, and fame have always been theirs. We tell ourselves, they're different from us; but are they?

Comedian and actress Whoopi Goldberg describes herself as having been a very quiet and dull child. Actor James Earl Jones, who is perhaps best known for the quality of his voice, once stuttered. Mariah Carey describes herself as an insecure child and says that she and her family sometimes had no place to stay. Michael Jordan couldn't get a date in high school. Actor and director Robert Townsend grew up without his dad in a tough neighborhood, while Quincy Jones, the musician and producer, never really knew what it was like to have a mother. Ronald McNair's early years were shaped in an environment designed to diminish his value through racial segregation, but that didn't stop him from becoming an astronaut. We could go on and on.

Success is not achieved without overcoming adversity or breaking down barriers. In *Stretch Your Wings* you will find quotations from people we all admire who had dreams and were determined to realize them; in other words, people who decided to stretch their wings and fly over the obstacles.

So what is your greatest ambition? What is the dream you long to achieve? What goals have you set? Now think about what things are keeping you down, holding you back, standing between you and the successful attainment of your goals. We hope that after reading this book you'll be inspired to write those obstacles down on a piece of paper, crumple the paper in your hands, and . . . you know what to do. That will be a first step toward stretching your wings.

Janet Cheatham Bell and Lucille Usher Freeman

ACKNOWLEDGMENTS

To my daughter, Kash'shawn Tyler Johnson, and my sons, Deavay Tyler Jr. and Donnavan P. Tyler. I love all of you so much more than words can express. Thank God for giving me the assignment of raising you. The three of you have truly been a blessing.

To my mother, Madora L. Usher, who has been there to encourage and inspire me. You've always reminded me that "This too shall pass" when life was challenging. You've sown seeds of time, wisdom, and love into the lives of your children and grandchildren. Thanks!

To my father, Robert L. Usher, who unselfishly supported us in our dreams and educational pursuits. You always made your four daughters feel special, and we could always count on you to be there through good times and bad.

I love you, Mom and Dad.

To my sisters, Patricia L. Holder, Roberta U. Fields, and Pauline U. Lampkin. You guys are the greatest! I'm at a loss for words (which is rare) in explaining how much you mean to me. Love you all.

To my brothers-in-law, Robert Holder Jr., Clinton B. Fields, and Derrick Lampkin. You have been like brothers.

To my nieces and nephews: Bobby, Jackie, Clinton, Sonya, Randy, Derrick, Michael, and SydneDion. The future belongs to you. Aim high. Dream big and step into it with confidence.

To my students (past and present). Wow, the lessons you've taught me have been countless. Thanks for letting me share your lives.

To my son-in-law, Kelvin Johnson. Thanks for all the technical support. You are truly a computer whiz!

To Rubie Stepney, Rachel Ray Moulder, Madearia King, Ruby L. Oliver, Henry and Audrey Locke, Brenda Miller, and Waymond H. Cobb Jr. Sometimes you just need someone to have faith and confidence in you. A heartfelt thanks!

To Janet Cheatham Bell. You are truly a great writer, coach, and friend.

To all of my friends and family members. You're loved and appreciated. Thanks for being there.

To Jadyn Alaura Johnson, my granddaughter and a little piece of heaven. You've already brought tremendous joy to the lives of those around you.

And finally, thanks, God. When we walk with you, all things are truly possible and we can toss out small plans.

Lucille Usher Freeman

Knowing Who I Am

What other people may be a little nervous to do and nervous to accept, I can do.

— **Lauryn Hill**

The real power behind whatever success I have now was something I found within myself—something that's in all of us, I think, a little piece of God just waiting to be discovered.

—**Tina Turner,** singer

I never did want to be normal.

—**Sinbad,** comedian and actor

I don't see anything the way you see it.... I don't take life seriously at all. I can't imagine taking it seriously.

—**Chris Rock,** comedian and actor

I was a very quiet and very dull child. I liked things other kids weren't into at the time—movies, theater, ballet.

—**Whoopi Goldberg,** comedian and actress

I've been called nerd, geek, every name in the book. I really didn't let it faze me. I'm no nerd. I'm just a person who is very determined in this life.

—**Woodlyne Jean-Charles,** seventeen-year-old Chicago student who won a gold medal in the NAACP Afro-Academic, Cultural, Technological and Scientific Olympics

Even [in high school] I was Eddie Murphy. I was voted most popular. I was like a little celebrity. I had already been on local cable; I was a hot shot. In high school I used to give assemblies. I did a show for the six grades over three days.... I did an hour of material about the school; impressions of teachers, students, hall monitors.... By the third day, people were sitting in the aisles. The truth is, I knew what I was put here to do.

—**Eddie Murphy,** comedian, actor, and producer

Singing was the one thing in my life that made me special; the one thing that transformed me from shy, awkward Patsy to cool, popular Patti. From an ugly duckling to a swan.

—**Patti LaBelle,** singer

I thought I was the tough chick of the school. But I think that stemmed from being insecure as a kid.

—**Mariah Carey,** singer-songwriter

Who I have become is who I have always tried to be.

—**Samuel Jackson,** actor

I was born in the slum, but the slum was not born in me.

—**Jesse Jackson,** special U.S. envoy to Africa

I believe in God, and so I believe in Mary Bethune.

—**Mary McLeod Bethune** (1875–1955), president, Bethune-Cookman College

No one has more confidence in me than I have in myself.

—**Allen Iverson,** basketball player, Philadelphia 76ers

I don't want to be like my dad. I just want to be like myself.

—**Jarrett Payton,** at age four, in response to a preschool teacher.
  His father is Hall of Fame football player Walter Payton.

Know who you are before they have to tell you.

—**Wolof proverb**

It's a painful process when you have to dig deep inside your-self and find out who you are. You have to be real honest with yourself and that was a process that took me a long time: find-ing out who I was, what I wanted, why I'm here.

—**Halle Berry,** actress

I've always known I was colored. When I was a Negro I knew I was colored; now that I'm Black I know which color it is. Any identity crisis I may have had never centered on race.

—**Nikki Giovanni,** poet

You show me one of these people who has been thoroughly brainwashed and has a negative attitude toward Africa, and I'll show you one who has a negative attitude about himself.

—**Malcolm X** (1925–1965), founder, Organization for Afro-American Unity

The fundamental way to make a slave is through deprivation; you take away what he is and what is his and replace it with another idea of who you want him to be.

—**Molefi Kete Asante,** former chairperson of African American Studies, Temple University

However far the stream flows, it never forgets its source.

—**Yoruba proverb**

When you hate yourself, you don't hear people say, "Gosh, you're smart," or, "You're a talented artist." Or if you hear them, you don't believe them.

—**Patrice Gaines,** *Washington Post* reporter

Everyone carries around his own monsters.

—**Richard Pryor,** comedian

When the static of self-doubt creeps in, the most important messages we can give ourselves are, "I'm lovable" and "I'm worthwhile."

—**Julia A. Boyd,** psychotherapist and author

When you have self-esteem, you will not allow anybody to relegate you to poverty or misery or unhappiness.

—**Maxine Waters,** U.S. congresswoman

Don't be afraid to feel as angry or as loving as you can, because when you feel nothing, it's just death.

—**Lena Horne,** singer and actress

I feel no flattery when people speak of my voice. I'm simply grateful that I found a way to work around my impairment. Once a stutterer, always a stutterer. If I get any credit for the way I sound, I accept it in the name of those of us who are impaired.

—**James Earl Jones,** actor

Who are you really? Who are you when nobody is looking? That is the real you.

—**T. D. Jakes,** speaker, minister, and author

The ultimate mystery is one's own self.

—**Sammy Davis Jr.** (1925–1990), singer, dancer, and actor

When I discover who I am, I'll be free.

—**Ralph Ellison** (1914–1994), author

I needed a lot of time and work to change my expectations of myself. I had to learn to believe that I could do anything I really wanted to do.

—**Wally "Famous" Amos,** entrepreneur

I am somebody! I may be poor, but I am Somebody! I may be on welfare but I am Somebody! I'm God's child. I must be respected and protected.

—Jesse Jackson, special U.S. envoy to Africa

I know it appears I have everything. And people think because you're on TV you have the world by a string. But I have struggled with my own self-esteem for many, many years. And I am just now coming to terms with it.

—Oprah Winfrey, host and owner, the *Oprah Winfrey Show*

People get really bent out of shape when I refer to myself as a multiracial person. I have to identify myself that way, because that's what I am. Not to say so would be inaccurate.

—Mariah Carey, singer-songwriter

Love affords wonder. And it is only love that gives [me] the liberty, the courage to go inside and see who am I really.

—**Maya Angelou,** poet and author

Being and Doing My Best

My responsibilities are to do the best work I can do and to be the best human being I can be....

— **Toni Morrison**

I always try my best. When I'm in a movie with veterans… who've won Academy Awards…I want to be able to hang, go where they're going, if not farther.…You've got to work with people who are better than you so you can rise to it.

—**Queen Latifah,** rap musician and actress

My mother raised me and my younger brother all by herself, so she really taught me independence and self-respect. She always encouraged me to believe in myself and told me that I could do anything I wanted to do.

—**Tevin Campbell,** singer

I don't want to be the best *black* golfer; I want to be the best golfer.

—**Tiger Woods,** golfer

I don't know how to sing black—and I don't know how to sing white, either. I know how to sing. Music is not a color to me. It's an art.

—**Whitney Houston,** singer and actress

I'm fanatical about high standards in every aspect of my work.

—**Jasmine Guy,** singer, dancer, and actress

I've been working hard toward a goal and that's to be the ultimate artist. An artist goes for perfection.

—**Usher,** singer and actor

When it became clear that people wanted a champion for the voices that were locked out, I decided to be that champion.

—**Carol Moseley-Braun,** former U.S. senator

With the gifts you have been given comes the responsibility to use and develop them.

—Les Brown, motivational speaker and author

I come from the kings and queens of Africa. I deserve the best. We all deserve the best. I'm not ashamed to say that I like the best in life, and I work hard every day to get it.

—Sean "Puffy" Combs, rap musician and producer

The healthiest competition occurs when average people win by putting in above-average effort.

—Colin Powell, chairperson, America's Promise—The Alliance for Youth

Be the best and they won't care who you are or what color you are. Be the best, and you will do well.

—Marc Hannah, cofounder, Silicon Graphics, Inc.

The idea is to win [and] you win the way you have to. Sometimes it's a good idea to save all your energy for the really tough battles.

—**Sugar Ray Robinson** (1921–1989), middleweight boxing champion

I really do believe that we can all become better than we are.

—**James Baldwin** (1924–1987), author

The Bible speaks of the priceless virtue of a good name. The Bible is right. All of us have the right to and the power to earn a good name through service and sacrifice and to help somebody other than ourselves.

—**Jesse Jackson Jr.,** U.S. congressman

Work on your reputation until it is established; when it is established, it will work for you.

—**Tunisian proverb**

[In high school], if there was an organization, I wanted to be the head of it. I wanted the best grades. I wanted to be the best everything.

—Halle Berry, actress

You've got to believe in yourself. The more you love and accept yourself, the sooner you'll be able to reach your goals.

—Florence Griffith Joyner (1959–1998), Olympic gold medalist

The minute you can develop yourself so you excel in whatever you do, then you are going to find that you don't have any real problems.

—S. B. Fuller (1905–1988), founder, Fuller Products Company

I never allowed myself to get lost, even when I was a little girl. I held on to the positive side. I never gave in to alcohol, never gave in to drugs, not even to smoking. I gave in to myself. I went inside of me to help me. It can happen. You can do it.

—**Tina Turner,** singer

I've hit 755 home runs, and I did it without putting a needle in my arm or a whiskey bottle in my mouth.

—**Hank Aaron,** former baseball player

When you realize that you can be your own best friend or your own worst enemy, then you stop blaming others and start to get out of the way of your own progress.

—**Louis Farrakhan,** leader of the Nation of Islam

Everybody loves a fool, but nobody wants him for a son.

—**Malinke proverb**

Anyone can talk, but you have to walk.

—**Venus Williams,** tennis champion

I'm prepared to cut anybody a lot of slack if they do something well.

—**Henry Louis Gates Jr.,** chairperson of Afro-American Studies,
  Harvard University

There's so many people who could be good, could be great, if they tried.… Some people are scared to risk it, though.

—**Charles Barkley,** basketball player, Houston Rockets

While everyone else is sleeping, I'm working.

—**Will Smith,** musician and actor

All work is honorable. Always do your best because someone is watching.

—Colin Powell, chairperson, America's Promise—The Alliance for Youth

Learn the craft of knowing how to open your heart and to turn on your creativity. There's a light inside of you.

—Judith Jamison, artistic director, Alvin Ailey American Dance Theater

The thing that makes you exceptional, if you are at all, is inevitably that which must also make you lonely.

—Lorraine Hansberry (1930–1965), playwright

I am me
proud as can be
I am success
I will strive to be the best

—Kimberly Dear, sixteen-year-old writer from Jacksonville, Florida

Family: Joy or **Nightmare?**

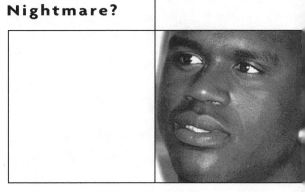

Thank goodness I had two parents who loved me enough to stay on my case.

— **Shaquille O'Neal**

The love and support I get from my family goes a long way, and helps me get through the hardest times.... For me, family is everything.

—**Monica,** singer

I never really knew what it was like to have a mother. There's no question that pushed me into a fantasy world. I used to sit for hours in the closet and just dream.

—**Quincy Jones,** musician and producer

My parents taught me a lot about life and a lot about the potholes in life. I'm more aware of where I am as a person because of that knowledge.

—**Michael Jordan,** businessman and former basketball player, Chicago Bulls

My parents have been behind me from the beginning. Their teachings assist me in almost every decision I make. They are my foundation.

—**Tiger Woods,** golfer

My mom was a single parent who raised five kids on the tough West Side of Chicago. She told us that we could do anything we wanted; we just had to work at it.

—**Robert Townsend,** actor, comedian, and director

My parents did their best to keep us out of harm's way. My mother outlined a code of conduct and strictly enforced it, to try and protect us. But her rules served an additional purpose. She was determined to put us on the path to a better life by teaching us to be disciplined, hardworking and responsible.

—**Jackie Joyner-Kersee,** Olympic gold medalist

My mom would say, "You might not be able to do things like a person who can see. But there are always two ways to do everything. You've just got to find the other way."

—**Ray Charles,** musician and singer

Yes, the reason I am what I am today is because I had a mother and father who cared enough to keep me in line, but who also always allowed me to dream my dreams.

—**Sinbad,** comedian and actor

There are individual personality traits of celebrities and sports stars and people whom I admire, but the only people I ever idolized are my parents.

—**Will Smith,** musician and actor

I've never felt celebrity status automatically makes you a role model. It's personal values, morals and ethics, not money and status. If it were [celebrity status], then my parents never would have been [my] role models.

—**Joe Dumars,** former basketball player, Detroit Pistons

[My parents] were comfortable with me exploring areas that they were not proficient in.

—**Mae Jemison,** former astronaut

Family is a mixed blessing. You're glad to have one, but it's also like receiving a life sentence for a crime you didn't commit.

—**Richard Pryor,** comedian

Parents and their parents are inflicted upon you in order to show what kind of person you are; what sort of world you live in and what the persons who dwell here need for their happiness and well being.

—W. E. B. DuBois (1868–1963), author and a founder of the NAACP

My mom is my hero. Our relationship is really, really close. If I do something wrong, I'll end up telling my mom because I feel I have to.

—Brandy, singer and actress

Growing up, I could always count on Momma to be my champion. Her constant encouragement formed my deep well of inspiration. I wanted to prove to her and everyone else that I had the ability to excel. I have approached every endeavor since then —athletic and otherwise—with that same sense of purpose.

—Jackie Joyner-Kersee, Olympic gold medalist

My mother was very protective and she was always telling me that you have to do well...because there are going to be people out there who are watching you and are not going to be very nice.

—Ilyasah Shabazz, daughter of Malcolm X and Betty Shabazz

My mother instilled in me that I could do anything I wanted to do. So I've never been afraid to try. When I see what I want, I don't see barriers.

—Morgan Freeman, actor

I would draw a circle on a piece of paper and my mother made me feel like Van Gogh.

—Damon Wayans, actor and comedian

[My mother] was very, very tough, a tough disciplinarian. Even when I was fifteen or sixteen, I had to be home by the time the streetlights went on. She saw to it I was exposed to a lot of things she couldn't afford....She was very intelligent. She is basically responsible for my success.

—**Denzel Washington,** actor

I was raised in a single-parent household and my mom worked jobs on the side to provide....She was *hard* on me and, though we laugh about it now, I tell her sometimes she was unnecessarily hard with her punishments.

—**Wesley Snipes,** actor

When my father died, he left his legacy, but he left nothing else. They expected [us] to go the welfare route, but my mother said no.

—**Gamilah Shabazz,** daughter of Malcolm X and Betty Shabazz

I don't think Daddy ever quite knew how to deal with me. And I didn't know how to deal with him either.

—**Diana Ross,** singer and actress

Of all those who changed my life, in looking back over the years, my biggest hero of all—in the end turned out to be my father, Pop. Not a day goes by that I don't appreciate what it means to have been his son.

—**Berry Gordy,** founder, Motown Industries

The glory of my boyhood years was my father. I loved him like no one in all the world.

—**Paul Robeson** (1898–1976), singer, actor, and political activist

My father seemed to [me] a figure of power. He had those rich Artistic Abilities, but he had more. He could fix anything that broke or stopped.... He could chuckle. No one has ever had, no one will ever have, a chuckle exactly like my father's.

—**Gwendolyn Brooks,** poet laureate, Illinois

The death of my father was a real big disappointment in life, but my stepfather, I love the guy. If I...should happen to die at an early age, I hope some guy will do as well for [my kids] as my stepfather has done for me.

—**Eddie Murphy,** comedian, actor, and producer

My grandmother paid my way through film school. She always had complete faith in me.

—**Spike Lee,** filmmaker

My grandmother taught me to count my blessings. There's always an upside to whatever bad happens.

—**Chamique Holdsclaw,** basketball player, Washington Mystics

It's difficult [to let your children learn on their own]. You know about so many things.... But you can't tell your son about it. He has to experience it for himself.... There's so much I want to tell him, but he can't see over those hills [of inexperience].

—**Walter Payton,** businessman, Hall of Fame football player, and former member of the Chicago Bears

Growing up, [my brother] was my idol.... Because of business we're not as close as we should be.... The brother relationship is more important than any records you could ever sell, any movies you could ever make. None of it can replace it. I'd give all that money back for my brother and me to be in love with each other like we were.

—**M.C. Hammer,** rap musician

It's generally true that people never allow their little brothers and sisters to grow up.

—**John Edgar Wideman,** author

I really believe that a man and a woman together, raising a family, is the purest form of happiness we can experience.

—**Will Smith,** musician and actor

The older you get, the smarter you realize your parents are.

—**Johnnie Cochran,** lawyer and talk show host

Relating To My Friends

Peer pressure is probably the biggest problem. Dealing with peers can be tough. Walking the straight and narrow while living the everyday life is hard for a lot of teens.

— Monica

Nonachievers in this world put great effort into helping others fail. In school they can produce a long list of names to call fellow students, such as "teacher's pet," "nerd" and "egghead." I suggest [that kids who are the targets of such ridicule] answer their critics this way: "Let's see what I am doing in twenty years and compare it with what you are doing. Then we'll know who made the right choice."

—Benjamin S. Carson, pediatric neurosurgeon and author

My dad taught me that being "good" doesn't make you weak —in fact, it means you are stronger.

—Sinbad, comedian and actor

I used to...want everything to go the way I thought it should go. But I've learned that you have to be together, but you have to be individuals and let each person be who she is.

—Salt, member of the musical group Salt-N-Pepa

Girlfriends are the best thing that ever happened to this planet.

—**Natalie Cole,** singer

The thing about fame that bothers me the most is that people no longer see you as a human being. I have bad days, too, days I just don't want to be bothered.

—**Jada Pinkett Smith,** actress

You owe it to others as well as to yourself to be very careful about letting others make up your mind for you.

—**Malcolm X** (1925–1965), founder, Organization for Afro-American Unity

Your peers are always the worst. They tease you or if you are playing a game, nobody wants to hold your hand because you have a brace on. I used to hate that. I think my way of getting back at them was through [excelling in] a sport.

—**Wilma Rudolph** (1940–1994), Olympic gold medalist

I don't know why [girls in elementary and junior high school] used to pick on me so much. I guess I was just "pickable."
—**Brandy,** singer and actress

Some people will tear you down just to see you fall. They'll do it even if your loss is their own.
—**Walter Mosley,** author

When people show you who they are, believe them the first time.
—**Maya Angelou,** poet and author

A close friend can become a close enemy.
—**Ethiopian proverb**

Choose to be with those who believe in you and encourage you to grow. Stay away from anyone who tears you down or always brings you the latest bad news.

—**Susan L. Taylor,** editor-in-chief, *Essence* magazine

Influence is a powerful thing. Be careful whom you allow to influence you.

—**T. D. Jakes,** speaker, minister, and author

I stay in touch with old friends. They aren't about to let me forget where I came from—not that I ever could.

—**Tyra Banks,** fashion model

Trying to go through life without friendship is like milking a bear to get cream for your morning coffee. It is a whole lot of trouble, and then not worth much after you get it.

—**Zora Neale Hurston** (1891–1960), anthropologist and author

Nobody, but nobody can make it out here alone.

—**Maya Angelou,** poet and author

[Our success is due to] prayer and unity and four creative minds willing to lay our differences aside to get things done.

—**Wanya Morris,** member of the singing group Boyz II Men

We must turn to each other and not on each other.

—**Jesse Jackson,** special U.S. envoy to Africa

We have to learn that we can agree to disagree without hurting and trashing each other.

—**Julia A. Boyd,** psychotherapist and author

I wasn't as nice a guy as I should have been all the time.…
And I don't have any excuses for that. I do have an explana-
tion, though—fear and ignorance.

—LL Cool J, rap musician and actor

I believe in recognizing every human being as a human being,
neither white, black, brown, nor red.

—Malcolm X (1925–1965), founder, Organization for Afro-American Unity

Get to know people whose lives are different from yours. Find
what you have in common with them.

—Kofi Annan, United Nations secretary-general

If you respect yourself, it's easier to respect other people.

—John Singleton, screenwriter and director

Doing the right thing when it is not popular or when it is not going to get everyone's approval is not always easy.

—**Benjamin S. Carson,** pediatric neurosurgeon and author

No person is your friend who demands your silence, or denies your right to grow.

—**Alice Walker,** poet and author

I would unite with anybody to do right and with nobody to do wrong.

—**Frederick Douglass** (1818–1895), abolitionist and orator

If you don't enjoy your own company, why would you expect someone else to enjoy being with you?

—**Iyanla Vanzant,** author and inspirational speaker

My mom [is] my manager and ... my best friend. ... She's paced
my whole career and my whole life.

—**Tyra Banks,** fashion model

You can never have too many people loving you and praying
for you.

—**George Foreman,** former heavyweight boxing champion

Am I Looking Good?

I wasn't a pretty boy growing up in Indianapolis, but the funny thing is, I've gotten more youthful-looking as I've gotten older. I don't do anything. Maybe confidence does it.

— Kenneth "Babyface" Edmonds

[In high school] I was very short, with a Napoleon complex.... So I had to overdo everything to overcompensate for being short.

—**Wesley Snipes,** actor

I was a homely little child. Just as funny-looking as I could be. When I heard Maya Angelou say how ugly she felt as a little girl, I wanted to call her right up and say, "Girlfriend, you too?"

—**Patti LaBelle,** singer

Like so many other people, I had to fight feeling ugly. We're all different, yet we're all the same.

—**Jasmine Guy,** singer, dancer, and actress

Just because you have money doesn't mean you can't feel worthless. Just because people consider you beautiful doesn't mean that *you* feel that way.

—**Janet Jackson,** singer

I think every woman has insecurities, no matter how success-ful you may be, no matter how public your life may be. We all have insecurities.

—**Tyra Banks,** fashion model

Our beauty has not been acknowledged, and the images of us have denigrated us.

—**Bebe Moore Campbell,** author

It's taken...years for there to be enough different-looking women in [Hollywood] for me to find my niche. They used to describe me as a moppet face and Raggedy Ann. Now there's lots of funny-faced women who are quite wonderful.

—**Whoopi Goldberg,** comedian and actress

If beauty is your only asset, don't come to Hollywood; here, beauty is a dime a dozen.

—**Vivica A. Fox,** actress

It will be marvelous when our culture succeeds in broadening its standard of beauty.

—**Joycelyn Elders,** former U.S. surgeon general

Most of my classmates were poor, but I was poorer than most —and I paid for it.... I wore homemade suits and pants. As if that wasn't enough, I was shy, insecure, and inarticulate, and I spoke in a thick down-home country brogue.... They... poke[d] fun at the country boy from Arkansas. They laughed at my "mammy-made" clothes.

—**John H. Johnson,** founder and CEO, Johnson Publishing Company

When Momma made me wear outfits she bought at the second-hand store, it was humiliating. They looked so old-fashioned. The dresses were all below the knee and dark-colored. The frills, puffs and long hemlines were a dead giveaway that they weren't new.

—**Jackie Joyner-Kersee,** Olympic gold medalist

Instead [of voting, building our own businesses and taking care of our people] we try to lighten our skin, straighten our hair, buy fancy clothes. We don't need new clothes; we need new ways of thinking.

—**Charles Evers,** former mayor of Fayette, Mississippi

There's nothing wrong with wanting a BMW or nice clothes. But BMW is not an advanced degree and a designer coat or jacket is not a life goal or worth a life.

—**Marian Wright Edelman,** founder and president, Children's

Defense Fund

My mother...taught me not to judge people by the amount of money they had or the kind of house they lived in or the clothes they wore. People should be judged, she told me, by the respect they have for themselves and others.

—**Rosa Parks,** seamstress who sparked the Montgomery, Alabama, bus boycott

When I was a child, it did not occur to me, even once, that the black in which I was encased would be considered, one day, beautiful....I had always considered it beautiful. I would stick out my arm, examine it, and smile.

—**Gwendolyn Brooks,** poet laureate, Illinois

My mother and father were very dark-skinned, and the color of the children ranged from black to dark brown. Color was never a problem in my family....We never felt sorry for ourselves because we were dark, and we accepted Africa as the home of our ancestors.

—**Benjamin E. Mays** (1895–1984), Morehouse College president

I was unique in that I was a kind of black that white people could accept. I was their daydream. I had the worst kind of acceptance because of the way I looked.

—**Lena Horne,** singer and actress

Even at my heaviest, I'm a fairly good-looking chick. Just because you're a big woman doesn't mean you're not…attractive.

—**Whoopi Goldberg,** comedian and actress

Imperfections make us perfect. The things we might not like, or that make us different from other people, are what make us very unique.

—**Iman,** fashion model

My makeup was like an American Express card to me—I never left home without it.

—**Patti LaBelle,** singer

We spend so much time and energy trying to fix ourselves and change ourselves and make up and rearrange ourselves. Energy that could be used in so many other ways to move ourselves forward.

—**Susan L. Taylor,** editor-in-chief, *Essence* magazine

Why are [we] willing to die for the sake of being thin?... We need to learn to love ourselves no matter how God designed us.

—**LouRedia Hannah,** kindergarten teacher from Tyler, Texas

I represent a black woman who is not afraid of who she is, [who doesn't] feel she has to alter or change herself to be what "society" wants.

—**Roshumba,** fashion model whose hair is short and natural

I can't understand the fuss. In my village there is no problem because we all look the same. Here there is so much difference in skin—so much is thought about it, and that's sad.

—**Alek Wek,** fashion model from Sudan, Africa

For me, being strong is a mental buildup. My body is my temple, and you have to take care of the body in order to take care of the mind. If you're physically strong, it's also exercise for your mind.

—**Jada Pinkett Smith,** actress

This thirty-four-year-old body just might have a few more years left [to play basketball]. Aging will eventually come, but you can sure slow it down. You'd be surprised what disciplined, consistent hard work will do.

—**Karl Malone,** basketball player, Utah Jazz

Exercise, like healthy eating, should be a lifelong habit.

—**Florence Griffith Joyner** (1959–1998), Olympic gold medalist

Every individual owes it to himself, and to the cause which he is serving, to keep a vigorous, healthy body.

—**Booker T. Washington** (1856–1915), founder, Tuskegee Institute

I can be out there sweating, yet when I finish my game, I'm dressed in a suit and heels.

—**Lisa Leslie,** basketball player, Los Angeles Sparks

Beauty is half a God-given favor; intelligence a whole one.

—**Fulani proverb**

What's Love Got To Do With It?

You've got to give meaning to your own life first. [A relationship] should not be seen as romantic fantasy.

—Jada Pinkett Smith

A lot of guys picked on me and they would do it in front of the girls. They would joke about my haircut, and the way I played with my tongue out, and just different things. And the girls would laugh at that. Right then I was dead. I couldn't get a date with anybody.

—**Michael Jordan,** businessman and former basketball player,
   Chicago Bulls

[As a young person, I was] socially retarded. I just had no clue of how you talk to girls.

—**Denzel Washington,** actor

I was a bit of a player, but it got played out. I got tired of lying and playing games and all that. I just got tired.

—**Coolio,** rap musician

As young men, we are raised to be players.... I was raised that way. I had to get it out of me.

—**M.C. Hammer,** rap musician

The problem with people in relationships the world over is when they want to get the person they love to love them, they think they have to be someone other than themselves. The secret to any relationship is just the opposite: being who you are.... So just be you.

—**Berry Gordy,** founder, Motown Industries

Be the selector not the selected. You do have control over who you date. Your selection from the start is important. What starts as a simple date could become a life-long relationship.

—**Roberta Fields,** educator and school counselor

If you are secure about who you are, you're less inclined to project feelings of inadequacy onto the other person.

—**Ava Muhammad,** Nation of Islam attorney

Before you can be in love and enjoy someone else, you have to love you. And the first step is knowing who you are. Every aspect, inside and out, of who you are is important.

—**Brenda Tapia,** founder and director, Love of Learning Program, Davidson College

The best way to be sure your beloved knows what you feel, what you want and what you need is to speak up and tell him as clearly as possible. And the best way to know what he's thinking is to ask.

—**Pearl Cleage,** author and playwright

If you don't like yourself, no one else will either. Why should they?

—**Michelle McKinney Hammond,** speaker and author

We cannot love other human beings without first loving and accepting ourselves.

—**Paula L. Woods and Felix H. Liddell,** authors

I used to think not having a father was no big deal. You don't really miss what you never had. But as I've gotten older I realize I have missed the influence of a father in my life and I think that's why I haven't…dealt with relationships with men very well because I was never sure how to.

—**Halle Berry,** actress

I learned it would be impossible for me to have a good relationship with anyone else until I have a good relationship with myself. I did not like me. I was not honest with myself. I did not want to be alone with me.

—**Iyanla Vanzant,** author and inspirational speaker

Dating is about spending time with someone you enjoy, not just about getting out of the house.

—**Sheneska Jackson,** author

I write songs about…the ups and downs of relationships [because] I know…what it feels like to hurt and be hurt.

—**Keith Sweat,** singer and producer

Listening to Sam Cooke and Antonio Carlos Jobim verified for me that [males] do have crazy romantic feelings, too.

—**Maxwell,** singer-songwriter and producer

If a fellow ceases dating you because you refuse to engage in the sexual act, you can be assured that he is not genuinely interested in you....Maintain your moral standards and improve your personality traits...and the right fellow will come along.

—**Martin Luther King Jr.** (1929–1968), civil rights leader and
   Nobel laureate

If our bodies are all we have to offer, we're in trouble.

—**Michelle McKinney Hammond,** speaker and author

Sex is a part of yourself that you should never give away on a whim.

—**Sheneska Jackson,** author

You know whom you love. You cannot know who loves you.

—**Yoruba proverb**

I had so much going for me, but I still thought I was nothing without a man.

—**Oprah Winfrey,** host and owner, the *Oprah Winfrey Show*

Nothing is more attractive to a man than a woman who knows what she wants.

—**Sheneska Jackson,** author

We all suffer from the preoccupation that there exists…in the loved one, perfection.

—**Sidney Poitier,** actor

Sometimes we try to overwhelm [someone] with the idea that "I am everything you could possibly need," so much that we actually devalue ourselves.

—**Ava Muhammad,** Nation of Islam attorney

I want someone who is going to cherish me. That's what I'm looking for.

—Vanessa Williams, singer and actress

There are deeper things than physical beauty that make you attractive to people. Long-lasting things. Things that aren't painted on your face or buttoned up your back....Things like the way you laugh, the way you love, the way you live your life.

—Patti LaBelle, singer

If you're not good company for yourself, you have to work to become the kind of person whose company you enjoy. If you enjoy your own company, there is no loneliness.

—Toni Morrison, Nobel laureate and author

Making Better Choices

I want to feel that I made choices that empowered me as a human being. My career is going to be here and gone. But I'm always going to be a human being. And I want to look myself in the mirror and say that I was the human being I wanted to be.

—Danny Glover

You have to stand for what you believe in. And sometimes you have to stand alone.

—**Queen Latifah,** rap musician and actress

I create my own calm. And I keep my balance, because I know that it's not really me, by myself....The Creator always gives me the energy.

—**Erykah Badu,** singer and businesswoman

As a teenager, I rebelled and wanted to break out of the confines of my strict upbringing. I'm not bragging, but I was in situations as a teenager where I could have easily ended up doing a lot of time.... My mother...would come out in the street and embarrass me.... She would come and get me. My partners would be laughing.... These are the same partners that are doing life now.

—**Denzel Washington,** actor

Change doesn't happen overnight.... Sometimes it takes years, particularly trying to remake yourself from your roots.

—**Patrice Gaines,** *Washington Post* reporter

Frankly, I have never cared too much what people say. What I am interested in is what they do.

—**Shirley Chisholm,** former U.S. congresswoman

I am not afraid to lift my head above the crowd, though I may draw criticism.

—**Dennis Kimbro,** author and director, Clark Atlanta University Center for Entrepreneurship

It takes no courage to get in the back of a crowd and throw a rock.

—**Thurgood Marshall** (1908–1993), Supreme Court justice

It's not enough to live. You must make your life mean something. You can't let fear hold you back…. You must ask yourself, "How have I made this world better?" And if you haven't made this world better yet, then start today. Right now. In some little way.

—**Charles Evers,** former mayor of Fayette, Mississippi

All young people need loyalty and discipline…. I found out to be loyal to something—a team, a family—changes your world.

— **George Foreman,** former heavyweight boxing champion

We all have ability. The difference is how we use it.

— **Stevie Wonder,** singer-songwriter and musician

I had the knowledge and power all the time but did not know how to use it…. I wasted time out of fear and ego. Other things kept me in a negative space. I now feel at peace.

—**The Artist Formerly Known As Prince,** singer-songwriter and musician

Sometimes we have so many things going on around us, with video games, radios blaring, television on, other people bustling around, that the hardest thing to do is just sit still.

—**Wynton Marsalis,** classical and jazz musician

Once I stopped dwelling on what I didn't have, on what I thought I was going to lose, and began to give freely, everything began to flow into my life.

—**Patti LaBelle,** singer

Sometimes it's not strategy…that makes the difference. It's whether a player really wants to take the shot. The only way you'll succeed is if you're not afraid of what will happen if you fail.

—**Mario Elie,** basketball player, San Antonio Spurs

You have to stop listening to all the "I can'ts" in life and just do it.... It always boils down to doing the work.

—**Dianne Houston,** director and screenwriter

I'm convinced that people like and enjoy helping those who are helping themselves.

—**Martin Luther King III,** president, Southern Christian Leadership Conference

Ninety-nine percent of the failures come from people who have the habit of making excuses.

—**George Washington Carver** (1864–1943), director of agricultural research, Tuskegee Institute

Putting off tough jobs makes them harder.

—**Marva Collins,** founder and director, Westside Preparatory School, Chicago

The greatest imprisonment of all and, therefore, the greatest freedom, too, is in your mind.

—**Patrice Gaines,** *Washington Post* reporter

I had to learn to tune out negative messages. For every success I've had in my life, there was someone telling me that I couldn't accomplish my goal. Like Langston Hughes said, you have to "hold fast to your dreams." For me that meant turning all those "nos" into "yeses."

—**Rolonda Watts,** entrepreneur and former talk show host

Never be limited by other people's limited imaginations.... If you adopt their attitudes, then the possibility won't exist [for you] because you'll have already shut it out.

—**Mae Jemison,** former astronaut

I had to make my own living and my own opportunity.... Don't sit down and wait for the opportunities to come; you have to get up and make them.

—**Madam C. J. Walker** (1867–1919), businesswoman

You have to make sacrifices in order to make progress.

—**Medgar Evers** (1925–1963), civil rights leader

Do what you feel is right.... There are going to be detractors [and] those who don't understand where you're going, but as long as you know you are doing the right thing...everything will work out.

—**Dexter King,** president, Martin Luther King, Jr. Center for Nonviolent Social Change

Pleasing yourself will draw you much closer to your goals than pleasing everybody else.

—**Dennis Kimbro,** author and director, Clark Atlanta University Center for Entrepreneurship

One thing my mother always emphasized for us was to go for the quality, try to take the high road in life.

—**Angela Bassett,** actress

You don't have to think about doing the right thing. If you're for the right thing, then you do it without thinking.

—**Maya Angelou,** poet and author

You can so outlive your past mistakes that even the most ardent critic will develop a warm respect for you.

—**Martin Luther King Jr.** (1929–1968), civil rights leader and Nobel laureate

Your attitude toward life doesn't affect the world and its inhabitants nearly as much as it affects you.

—**Dennis Kimbro,** author and director, Clark Atlanta University Center for Entrepreneurship

People are always telling me that I'm lucky, but…I made some of my luck. I made it by working hard and trusting the logic of events, which always favor the bold and the active and the prepared.

—**John H. Johnson,** founder and CEO, Johnson Publishing Company

It is always better to form the habit of learning how to see things for yourself, listen to things for yourself, and think for yourself; then you are in a better position to judge for yourself.

—**Malcolm X** (1925–1965), founder, Organization for Afro-American Unity

What About Racism?

I have fought against white domination, and against black domination. I have cherished the ideal of a society in which all persons live together in harmony. It is an ideal I hope to live for and achieve and it is an ideal for which I am prepared to die.

— Nelson Mandela

We didn't set out to grab a black or white audience, but to grab anyone who wanted to listen. I would hope we cross over to blacks, whites, Asians, people all over the world. Music is not for a specific race; it's universal.

—**Nathan Morris,** member of the singing group Boyz II Men

Because I want every kid to be viewed as a person rather than as a member of a certain race does not mean that I'm not black enough. . . . Do they want me to be positive just for black kids and negative for everybody else?

—**Michael Jordan,** businessman and former basketball player,
  Chicago Bulls

For the first nine years of my life, I was hanging out with white people at school and black people at home. I just really learned how to deal with everybody. I don't look at it as a white-black thing.

—**Will Smith,** musician and actor

People are nice to each other and they're also mean to each other. That's the way it's always been and probably always will be. The fact that we're different colors is basically just an excuse for doing that.

—**Richard Pryor,** comedian

When we all learn about our history, about how much we've accomplished while being handicapped with RACISM, it can only inspire us to greater heights.

—**Spike Lee,** filmmaker

Americans such as myself...have to suffer the indignity of being reminded time and time again that at one point in this country's history we were human chattel, we were property, we could be traded, bought and sold. I would like to put a stake through the heart of this Dracula.

—**Carol Moseley-Braun,** former U.S. senator

There's nothing sweeter or more precious than the secrets buried in our history.

—**Walter Mosley,** author

Every day we got the same message drummed into us. "Despite discrimination and lynch mobs," teachers told us, "some black folks have always managed to find a way to succeed."

—**Arthur Ashe** (1943–1993), tennis player and author

We are the only [ethnic] group within the United States ever forbidden by law to read and write.

—**Alice Childress,** playwright and author

Black people are on probation in America. We have been since 1865.

—**Bebe Moore Campbell,** author

[During] my childhood...I received strong messages about the worth and abilities of my people....None of [the] positive aspects of my childhood, however, provided refuge from racism.
—**Johnnetta B. Cole,** former president, Spelman College

Don't believe those people who say you're inferior because you're black. [If] you're inferior [it's] because you can't get the books to read, and you can't get the teachers to teach you.
—**John Hope Franklin,** professor emeritus of history, Duke University

Equality might be denied, but I *knew* I was not inferior.
—**Paul Robeson** (1898–1976), singer, actor, and political activist

Let [racism] be a problem to someone else....Let it drag them down. Don't use it as an excuse for your own shortcomings.
—**Colin Powell,** chairperson, America's Promise—The Alliance for Youth

Football is probably no different from any other avenue in life. My dad went through [racial discrimination] when he first started....You have to keep pushing and keep working and eventually good things happen.

—**Tony Dungy,** head coach, Tampa Bay Buccaneers

I was a Negro for twenty-three years. I gave that...up. No room for advancement.

—**Richard Pryor,** comedian

Hated by whites and being an organic part of the culture that hated him, the black man grew in turn to hate in himself that which others hated in him.

—**Richard Wright** (1908–1960), author

The price of hating other human beings is loving oneself less.

—**Eldridge Cleaver** (1936–1998), minister of information, Black Panther Party

Black anger always, in a way, flatters white power.

—**Shelby Steele,** educator and author

For a long time, I was the only black female music-video direc-tor, but it never occurred to me to feel disadvantaged. Now I'm one of the few black female film directors in a racist, sexist busi-ness, but nothing is gonna stop me!

—**Millicent Shelton,** writer and director

The predominant image of blacks in films is still "ghetto." I would like to produce quality films that tell interesting stories and reflect our true diversity.

—**Tracie Kemble,** vice-president of development, HBO's NYC Productions

You will *never* hear me say I don't see myself as a black actor but just an actor who happens to be black. Every chance I get I'm going to tell you I'm an African-American man who is acting. I'm going to let you know and I will not allow anybody to say otherwise....I have a passionate love for African people and culture.

—**Wesley Snipes,** actor

Blacks have been rejected so much, that they've gotten into the habit of rejecting themselves. The internal barriers are much more difficult to overcome than the external ones.

—**Dwayne Kennedy,** comedian

Without realizing it, we'd been taught to hate ourselves and love white people, and it was causing us to self-destruct.

—**Nathan McCall,** author

The mind becomes the last plantation.

—**Itabari Njeri,** contributing editor, *Los Angeles Times Magazine*

I hope that one day people of all colors will be able to walk in any neighborhood without automatic suspicion. But until then, it's important that those of us who experience prejudice refuse to regard it as an acceptable response.

—**R. Kelly,** singer-songwriter

[When minorities are the majority,] will…America be any different from the country we live in today? The answer completely depends on whether whites, blacks, Latinos, Asians and Native Americans find common ground together—or common enemies in one another.

—**Farai Chideya,** reporter, ABC News

The fact that we have endured wrongs and hardships which would have destroyed any other race, and have increased in numbers and public consideration, ought to strengthen our faith in ourselves and our future.

—**Frederick Douglass** (1818–1895), abolitionist and orator

I am trying to get our people to see that their color does not hold them back as much as they think.

—**George Washington Carver** (1864–1943), director of agricultural research, Tuskegee Institute

If anybody's going to help African-American people, it's got to be ourselves.

—**Earvin "Magic" Johnson,** businessman and former basketball player, Los Angeles Lakers

The best investment we can make is in our people.

—**LaVan Hawkins,** businessman

Staying Safe

I'm afraid *all the time*....But none of [my] fears rule my life. Fear is a breeding ground for fear. If you don't control it, it will control you.

—Queen Latifah

We have to stop pimping each other, robbing each other, doggin' each other, and not trusting each other and killing each other.... The biggest threat to the black man today is not the white man but the black man. The black man continues to self-destruct.

— **M.C. Hammer,** rap musician

When natural energies and hungers have no healthy outlet, they feed on their hosts, attack friends and family, the physical environment.... What gets torn up is what you can get your hands on.

—**John Edgar Wideman,** author

It's time for all young people...to stop the violence, drugs and crime from messing up their lives and our communities. We have to take responsibility for our own actions, and set good examples for the little kids coming up. They have to learn early that violence is a dead end and has to be stopped before it kills us all.

—**Monica,** singer

The only way that we will disappear, become extinct, is if we kill ourselves.

—Maya Angelou, poet and author

We must rebuild our communities, but first we must rebuild our minds.

—Bebe Moore Campbell, author

Fear is the great motivator and the great equalizer. Fear will make a brave man a coward and a coward, brave.

—W. Kamau Bell, comedian

You have to eat, rest and figure out a way to handle your fear.

—Morgan Freeman, actor

[Whining] is not only uncomfortable and miserable. It also alerts the brute.

—**Maya Angelou,** poet and author

The emotional repression in the black community is a time bomb ticking in our faces.

—**Kevin Powell,** author

Anger is a problem when you don't see an end to it, when you can't control it....The heaviest burden in our community now is this unfocused, unchanneled anger—toward each other, toward white folks, toward the system.

—**Bebe Moore Campbell,** author

I've made so many mistakes....I was always one of the brothers trying to be a gangster with all the other kids because I didn't want them to think I was soft, although I was.

—**Kirk Franklin,** gospel musician

Hungry people cannot be good at learning or producing anything, except perhaps violence.

—Pearl Bailey (1918–1990), actress

The most dangerous creation of any society is that man who
has nothing to lose.

—James Baldwin (1924–1987), author

Rage doesn't need reason. It only needs targets.

—Clarence Page, *Chicago Tribune* columnist

Strong family units will make strong and secure neighborhoods.

—Shirley Chisholm, former U.S. congresswoman

Hard work is the way....Don't try to take the easy way out. Leave the drugs alone; no matter how great they might make you feel, they really have their side effects and sooner or later, they'll catch up to you.

—**Marlon Wayans,** comedian and actor

You know what's wrong with today's kids, why there's so much shooting today? The kids today have too much stuff. We didn't have anything worth killing anybody for in the seventies. Nobody wanted your raggedy jacket. You never saw anybody killed over a Kmart jacket. "Gimme your raggedy no-zip-it-up jacket!" You'd say, "Here, take it. I was hoping somebody would get this jacket."

—**Sinbad,** comedian and actor

If you don't believe you are anything other than a consumer, you will understand how it is possible to kill someone over a jacket.

—**Toni Morrison,** Nobel laureate and author

To the degree that I harm my brother, no matter what he is doing to me, to that extent I am harming myself.

—**Martin Luther King Jr.** (1929–1968), civil rights leader and
    Nobel laureate

We wouldn't be killing each other if we knew who we were.

—**Brenda Tapia,** founder and director, Love of Learning Program,
    Davidson College

I think about the child abuse, dropping out of school, sleeping on the subways, carrying guns, using drugs, abusing sex. And I realize that only God could leave me standing where I am today.

—**LL Cool J,** rap musician and actor

If you are wise and strong enough to survive the threatening atmosphere of the streets, then channel that same energy into thriving in the same atmosphere at your school.

—**Bill Cosby,** comedian

War will stop when we no longer praise it, or give it any attention at all. Peace will come wherever it is sincerely invited.

—**Alice Walker,** poet and author

Money, Money, Money

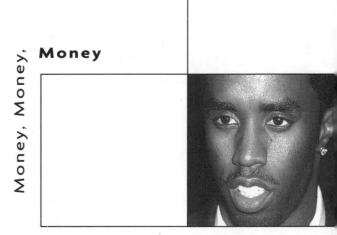

My motivation has not been money. My motivation has always been to entertain people, make people feel good. That's what helps me be a workaholic; that's what helps me stay up late at night. I love performing for people.

— Sean "Puffy" Combs

Money and things never belong to anyone. They just come and go and come again. That's how I see it.

—**Will Smith,** musician and actor

I realized as a kid I could be rich.

—**Evander Holyfield,** heavyweight boxing champion

The real question isn't if I'm worth $120 million; it's, if somebody can afford to pay me $120 million, how much is *he* making?

—**Shaquille O'Neal,** basketball player, Los Angeles Lakers

It's not what you're worth, it's what you can negotiate.

—**John Salley,** former basketball player

I don't play this game for money. People come out to watch you play, not to count your money.

—**Kevin Garnett,** basketball player, Minnesota Timberwolves

We don't have to be entertainers, athletes or drug dealers to make money in this country.... The great fortunes are made in business.

—**Maceo Sloan,** CEO, Sloan Financial Group, Durham, North Carolina

I think from success you'll gain access.... I don't think black folks need unity as much as they need industry.... We have to start opening businesses.

—**Keenen Ivory Wayans,** producer, screenwriter, director, and actor

"Have blacks finally arrived in Hollywood?" It depends on what we produce. The bottom line is that you have to make money. Then nobody cares what color you are. When you do something important and make money—you've arrived, man.

—**Quincy Jones,** musician and producer

I wanted to start my own business because I wanted to save money for my college education.

—**Daniel Miller Jr.,** ten-year-old business owner

With all this acting, I try to find roles where I'll walk away with something more than just the paycheck.

—**Regina Taylor,** playwright and actress

The most menial job is never beneath our dignity, but rather an opportunity to love and serve joyfully.

—**Susan L. Taylor,** editor-in-chief, *Essence* magazine

I suppose that every boy and every girl born in poverty have felt at some time in their lives the weight of the world against them. What people...did not expect them to do it was hard for them to convince themselves that they could do.

—**Booker T. Washington** (1856–1915), founder, Tuskegee Institute

A man's bread and butter is only insured when he works for it.

—**Marcus Garvey** (1887–1940), founder, Universal Negro Improvement Association

You will find it the fashion in the America where eventually you will live and work, to judge…life's work by the amount of money it brings you. This is a grave mistake. The return from your work must be the satisfaction which that work brings you….Income is not greenbacks, it is satisfaction; it is creation; it is beauty.

—**W. E. B. DuBois** (1868–1963), author and a founder of the NAACP

Find out what you love to do, and then figure out how to make money doing it.

—**Pat Campbell,** diversity marketing strategic planner, Mobil Oil Corporation

My object in life is not simply to make money for myself or to spend it on myself. I love to use a part of what I make in trying to help others.

—**Madam C. J. Walker** (1867–1919), businesswoman

I want to own my stuff. I want to get into the type of economic power that other ethnic groups have.

—**Sean "Puffy" Combs,** rap musician and producer

Money is not the key. Money makes life easier, but money is not what gives you success. Integrity, dignity, self-respect; that is success.

—**Sinbad,** comedian and actor

While many believe that only the wealthy have economic power, all of us have the power to spend our money where we choose, whether we're making a million-dollar purchase or buying a box of detergent.

—**Camille Cosby,** philanthropist and entrepreneur

It's very easy in this physical and material society to be totally out of touch with yourself.

—**Brenda Tapia,** founder and director, Love of Learning Program,
   Davidson College

We must love ourselves back to emotional health first, and then economic well-being.

—**Bebe Moore Campbell,** author

If you live a life of service, you don't have to worry about money. Money will come.

—**Robert Shaw Logan,** owner, Logan Enterprises, Saluda, South Carolina

Learning All I Can

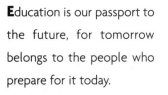

Education is our passport to the future, for tomorrow belongs to the people who prepare for it today.

— **Malcolm X**

If you can't count, they can cheat you.
If you can't read, they can beat you.

—**Toni Morrison,** Nobel laureate and author

Homework is something that's got to be done.

—**Monica,** singer

If I had it to do over again, I wouldn't have dropped out of high school, especially just one semester shy of graduation. As an adult, not having that diploma did a number on my head many times. Frankly, it often made me feel insecure, sometimes downright inferior. As a teenager, though, I couldn't see that far down the road. All I cared about was the moment.

—**Patti LaBelle,** singer

In college I learned responsibility. Some days you open a book and say, "I can't do this, I got a headache." Then the little bell rings in your head and you say, "I got to."

—**Bo Jackson,** former baseball and football player

I've always told the musicians in my band to play what they know and then play above that. Because then anything can happen, and that's where great art and music happens.

—**Miles Davis** (1926–1991), jazz musician

You've got to know the business [of entertaining] before you become an entertainer. Otherwise, you can have all the fame in the world and still be broke.

—**Missy Elliott,** owner, The Gold Mind, Inc., a music production company

I have attained quite a few goals in my own life but I am the same person, with the same brain, that I was when no one else shared the academic bottom of my fifth-grade class with me.

—**Benjamin S. Carson,** pediatric neurosurgeon and author

I had to be tough, I had to be hard core when it came to my grades because I knew that I definitely needed something that …would help me stand out.…You had to be a shining star or else people would just overlook you.

—**Cedric Jennings,** graduate of Brown University and subject of the book *A Hope in the Unseen: An American Odyssey from the Inner City to the Ivy League*

Chess is a proven way for you to learn to concentrate better; [it] enhances creativity, critical-thinking skills, memory, problem solving, intellectual maturity, self-esteem, and even increases academic achievement.

—**Maurice Ashley,** chess grandmaster

Young black[s] need to get an education.... There is so much emphasis on athletics that the value of an education gets pushed to the background. Athletics should be a means to obtain an education, not the other way around. Development of one's mind is much more important than anything.

—**Bo Jackson,** former baseball and football player

It's amazing how schools give more glory to their ballplayers—trophies for the ballplayers and a little button for the debate team.

—**Jawanza Kunjufu,** president, African American Images, a publishing company

Though you will be surrounded by those who say that education doesn't count or excellence doesn't matter, believe me, they do.... Hard work produces good results. Dumb people run absolutely nothing.... Poverty can be overcome and one individual can make a difference.

—**L. Douglas Wilder,** former governor of Virginia

My confidence is in knowing that I have probably trained harder than anyone I am going to run against.

—**Michael Johnson,** Olympic gold medalist and author

Wisdom is not like money to be tied up and hidden.

—**Akan proverb**

The purpose of education...is to create in a person the ability to look at the world for himself, to make his own decisions.

—**James Baldwin** (1924–1987), author

Organized education gives us general information, but there are things we have to learn by ourselves.

—**Lauryn Hill,** singer and rap musician

One's work may be finished some day, but one's education never.

—**Alexandre Dumas, père** (1802–1870), French novelist and playwright

Language became an obsession with me. I began to realize the meaning and the power of words.

—**Malcolm X** (1925–1965), founder, Organization for Afro-American Unity

My own perception of Malcolm bordered on fascination.... Here was a man who in the 8th grade in Michigan, at a school where I think he was the only black in his class and one of the very few in the school, had been a straight-A student, and in fact the president of his class. Obviously he had to be exceptional to be those things.

—**Alex Haley** (1921–1992), author

Education empowers you.

—**Camille Cosby,** philanthropist and entrepreneur

Education...is the key to our salvation. Knowledge is power.

—**Johnnie Cochran,** lawyer and talk show host

People who think education is expensive have never counted the cost of ignorance.

—**Andrew Young,** former mayor of Atlanta

Since new developments are the products of a creative mind, we must therefore stimulate and encourage that type of mind in every way possible.

—**George Washington Carver** (1864–1943), director of agricultural research, Tuskegee Institute

Always know there is unlimited power in a developed mind and a disciplined spirit. If your mind can conceive it and your heart can believe it, you can achieve it.

—**Jesse Jackson,** special U.S. envoy to Africa

What makes one an intellectual is the drive to learn, to question, to understand, to criticize, not as a means to an end but as an end in itself.

—Stephen L. Carter, law professor, Yale University

I would go to the library and borrow scores by all those great composers....Knowledge is freedom and ignorance is slavery, and I just couldn't...be that close to freedom and not take advantage of it.

—Miles Davis (1926–1991), jazz musician

From the time that I can remember having any thoughts about anything, I recall that I had an intense longing to learn to read.

—Booker T. Washington (1856–1915), founder, Tuskegee Institute

Books showed me there were possibilities in life, that there were actually people like me living in a world I could not only aspire to but attain. Reading gave me hope. For me it was the open door.

—**Oprah Winfrey,** host and owner, the *Oprah Winfrey Show*

The impulse to dream had been slowly beaten out of me by experience. Now it surged up again and I hungered for books, new ways of looking and seeing.

—**Richard Wright** (1908–1960), author

Good books are good nutrition
A reader is a Guest
nourished, by riches of the Feast,
to lift, to launch, and to applaud
the world.

—**Gwendolyn Brooks,** poet laureate, Illinois

I developed an appetite for biographies and autobiographies, a hunger to know how other people lived their lives—specifically, how they overcame obstacles and challenges.

—**Patrice Gaines,** *Washington Post* reporter

I have observed a simple fact about the influence of books. Students who excel academically, read extensively. I suspect there is a one-to-one correlation between avid reading and intellectual accomplishments.

—**Benjamin S. Carson,** pediatric neurosurgeon and author

I resented the way I was treated by some students, and I decided to retaliate the only way I knew how—by beating them in class and in extracurricular activities....I studied harder, partly because I didn't have enough money to take girls out, and partly because I wanted to even the score.

—**John H. Johnson,** founder and CEO, Johnson Publishing Company

Experiencing great things can motivate us to want to be great ourselves. Whatever the achievement that inspires us may be, we have to realize that it takes many long hours of practicing to become good, let alone great.

—**Wynton Marsalis,** classical and jazz musician

Hold Fast **To Dreams**

I have come to know that God can dream a bigger dream for you than you can dream for yourself....

— Oprah Winfrey

Following your dream is so important.

—**Wanya Morris,** member of the singing group Boyz II Men

I'm *living* my dream and not *wishing* for it anymore.

—**Kobe Bryant,** basketball player, Los Angeles Lakers

When I was still a very small child, I remember sneaking off by myself and entering into my own little world of entertainment. I would stand up in front of the mirror in a trance, watching my lips move and my body sway as I sang along with an Etta record like "Dance With Me, Henry," performing for a wildly cheering imaginary audience. At those times, I felt alive and in my element.

—**Diana Ross,** singer and actress

[At age twelve] I stood up on a little chair and sang [my first solo in church]....I traveled from about the age of thirteen to sixteen with my dad, singing with...real gospel giants. It was great training.

—**Aretha Franklin,** singer

I was in high school when I began thinking about becoming an actor.

—**Cuba Gooding Jr.,** actor

When I was growing up in Florida, I had a very limited picture of the possibilities. I didn't know anybody who was an actor.... I've learned that the world is bigger than the south side of St. Petersburg....This career has already been more than I ever expected.

—**Angela Bassett,** actress

I always tell young people like me to pursue their dreams. I tell them, "You can do it, and never say you can't."

—**Andrea Gardiner,** first African American to win the U.S. Junior Ladies
Figure Skating Championship

I know how to go out there and make people laugh. I've been doing it since I was a teenager. I trust my instincts.

—**Eddie Murphy,** comedian, actor, and producer

When I got my first job in New Orleans playing in a honky-tonk … I was seventeen, and it was the same as Carnegie Hall to me.

—**Louis Armstrong** (1901–1971), jazz musician

I've gotten to where I've gotten because I had the chance to dream, and I want to instill that in kids. All kids have a spark in them. Somebody just needs to ignite that spark. They can accomplish anything.

—**Sean "Puffy" Combs,** rap musician and producer

In class, I stumbled through math, fumbled through physics, and...even enjoyed geology. [However], all I ever looked forward to was ROTC.

—**Colin Powell,** chairperson, America's Promise—The Alliance for Youth

If you'd told me in college that within a year my face would be all over the world and millions of people would know my name, I'd have said you were crazy.

—**Michael Jordan,** businessman and former basketball player, Chicago Bulls

I always assumed I would go into space ever since I was a little girl. I would have applied to be an astronaut if there had never been a single person going into space.

—**Mae Jemison,** former astronaut

I like to think that acting picked me. I didn't really pick acting. I wanted to be a basketball player. I wanted to be a doctor. I can't really say why I act. I just do. I always have. Why does Michael Jordan play basketball the way he does? Because he can.

—**Laurence Fishburne,** actor

I've accepted my reality. . . . I was meant to sound the way I do.

—**Kathleen Battle,** opera singer

I didn't have much to say about it. It had to be. I didn't choose music. Music chose me.

—**Marian Anderson** (1902–1993), opera singer

Yes, I do believe that God has sent every man and every woman into the world to do something unique and something distinctive, and if he or she does not do it, it will never be done.

—**Benjamin E. Mays** (1895–1984), Morehouse College president

Failure to recognize possibilities is the most dangerous and common mistake one can make.

—**Mae Jemison,** former astronaut

An artist must be free to choose what he does, certainly, but he must also never be afraid to do what he might choose.

—**Langston Hughes** (1902–1967), poet

I believe that art is an expression of what people feel and want.

—**Romare Bearden** (1912–1988), artist

We have to change the erroneous assumption that you have a better chance of being Magic Johnson than you do of being a brain surgeon.

—**Henry Louis Gates Jr.,** chairperson of Afro-American Studies, Harvard University

No skill or vocation is the white man's exclusive province.

—Reginald F. Lewis (1942–1993), CEO, TLC Beatrice International
Holdings, Inc.

This new world will be one of mind-boggling methodologies, technologies and tools of hope.... Technology will not care about the color of our skin, or the condition of our poverty. It will care only about our ability and the quality of our information and education.

—Percy Sutton, cofounder and board chairperson, Inner City
Broadcasting, New York City

We decided long ago that we must prepare students to take advantage of every opportunity related to the business industry. And these golf courses are the places where business is generally done.

—Sybil Mobley, dean of the business school at Florida A&M University,
Tallahassee

[If you want to be an entrepreneur,] think, then strategize. If you're not a thinker, then surround yourself with people who are.

—**Phillip Jones,** chairperson and CEO, Intellectual Properties

Management, Inc., Atlanta

I was a dreamer. I just felt there was no limit to what people could do or how far they could go. . . . I wanted Broadway. I wanted movies. I wanted television.

—**Berry Gordy,** founder, Motown Industries

It took from the time I was seventeen . . . 'til I was forty-five to make the decision that [art] was what I really wanted to do. I couldn't live the rest of my life without doing it.

—**Ed Dwight,** sculptor

The thing which has been the secret of whatever I have done is the fact that I have been able to earn a living by doing the work which I wanted to do and work that the world needed done.

—**W. E. B. DuBois** (1868–1963), author and a founder of the NAACP

Success is not the key to happiness. Happiness is the key to success. If you love what you are doing, you will be successful.

—**Herman Cain,** CEO, Godfather Pizza

Tell our children they're not going to jive their way up the career ladder. They have to work their way up hard. There's no fast elevator to the top.

—**Marian Wright Edelman,** founder and president, Children's Defense Fund

I'm a workaholic. I feel that when I wake up in the mornings, if I'm not working, attending acting class, going to the gym … the world is passing me by. Whatever this rat race is about, I'm a part of it. I'm one of the rats!

—Iman, fashion model

The large monster of practicing always comes to trample on our dreams of becoming great without sacrifice. Almost no one likes to practice.... We all want to be heroes, but we just don't want to fight the dragon. And that is understandable. Dragons have bad breath.

—Wynton Marsalis, classical and jazz musician

Hold fast to dreams
For if dreams die
Life is a broken-winged bird
That cannot fly.

—Langston Hughes, (1902–1967), poet

Hanging In There

I've missed more than nine thousand shots in my career. Twenty-six times I've been trusted to take the game winning shot and missed. I've failed over and over and over again in my life. And that is why I succeed.

—Michael Jordan

Nothing in this world comes without a price. This is one truth that I've sung and that I've lived.

—**Gladys Knight,** singer

I don't know what it is about me, but I think I was born to go through terrible things and then survive them.

—**Natalie Cole,** singer

You're going to succeed and you're going to fail. It's what you do when you fail. If you bounce back, it's going to make you that much better....If you always succeed, it would be a dream,...not reality.

—**Grant Hill,** basketball player, Detroit Pistons

I believe the Lord doesn't put any weight on your shoulders he doesn't feel you can carry.

—**Heavy D,** rap musician

If something doesn't work, don't give up, go a different direction.

—Edward G. Gardner, cofounder Soft Sheen hair care products, Chicago

I will not leave South Africa, nor will I surrender. The struggle is my life. I will continue fighting for freedom until the end of my days.

—Nelson Mandela, former president of South Africa

You can win if you got the heart and tenacity and soul to keep on trying.

—Miles Davis (1926–1991), jazz musician

[My family] moved all over Long Island and New York.... There were times when we didn't have a place to live and we stayed with [my mother's] friends. Those were very frightening periods.

—Mariah Carey, singer-songwriter

When you're forced to move around a lot, you're either going to become introverted,...or you learn to extend yourself and reach out to people.

—**Blair Underwood,** actor

Nothing is ever permanent.

—**Jacob Lawrence,** artist

God is just. He deposits just as much genius in housing projects as he does in the suburbs. Just as many lawyers and legislators and state directors can and have been born in sharecroppers' shacks as in penthouses and high-income neighborhoods.

—**Michael Thurmond,** state welfare director, Georgia

We are all born into different circumstances, and yet our concerns are mostly the same, at least at the core: we all want self-respect, self-reliance, self-indulgence. Maybe your mother's a crack addict, or your father can't hold a job. Or maybe it's not cool where you are to do well in school or to work for a better future. It all amounts to the same thing.... You've got to pick yourself up, scrape yourself off and move forward.

—**Montel Williams,** talk show host

Only a man who knows what it is like to be defeated can reach down to the bottom of his soul and come up with the extra ounce of power it takes to win when the match is even.

—**Muhammad Ali,** former heavyweight boxing champion

I see my painful experiences in life as stepping-stones.

—**Diana Ross,** singer and actress

I have been creative, constantly taking chances—racehorse chances—to negotiate my path. I have used a number of ploys to erect my own bridges over boiling waters, laughing when I wasn't tickled and scratching when I didn't itch. And I am here— still here, despite the odds.

—**Maya Angelou,** poet and author

Put that smile on your face and keep living.

—**Earvin "Magic" Johnson,** businessman, former basketball player, Los Angeles Lakers

I...like the fact that [Eartha Kitt] didn't let anyone stop her. She would say, "I may be a woman and I may be black, but that's not going to stop me from reaching my goal in life." I admire that in anyone.

—**Toni Braxton,** singer

We have too many youngsters who are quitting before the race is even begun.

—**Colin Powell,** chairperson, America's Promise—The Alliance for Youth

We have it in our power to convert the weapons intended for our injury into positive blessings.

—**Frederick Douglass** (1818–1895), abolitionist and orator

Mama and I agreed that if I didn't make it [as a baseball player], I'd come back and finish my education. I had no intention of not making it.

—**Hank Aaron,** former baseball player

Don't give up—keep your dreams. Don't let anybody tell you that you can't do something. If you want something bad enough, work for it.

—**Kelton "LDB" (Little Drummer Boy) Kessee,** member of the music
   group Immature

Failure is the really bad "F-word."...It's something you can't be afraid of, because you'll stop growing....The next step beyond failure could be your biggest success in life.

—**Debbie Allen,** choreographer, actress, producer, and director

Life is pretty much like [a] bicycle. We all need balance, know-how, and a sense of confidence. Life can become wobbly at times, and sometimes we may fall, but we should never let one fall deter us from getting on that bicycle again.

—**Marva Collins,** founder and director, Westside Preparatory School,
   Chicago

One faces down fears of today so that those of tomorrow might be engaged.

—**Alice Walker,** poet and author

When I look back at my childhood…I see that I was a ripe candidate for low self-esteem as an adult. There were low periods…when I failed the third grade because of lengthy absences for illness and the kids poked fun at me.

—**Julia A. Boyd,** psychotherapist and author

When the going gets tough and you feel like throwing your hands in the air, listen to that voice that tells you "Keep going. Hang in there." Guts and determination will pull you through.

—**Alice Coachman,** Olympic gold medalist

A problem is a chance for you to do your best.

—**Duke Ellington** (1899–1974), jazz musician

Thinking your way through your problem is better than wishing your way through.

—**Coleman Young** (1918–1997), mayor of Detroit

The way I look at problems is to try to see if the past teaches us anything,

—**John Hope Franklin,** professor emeritus of history, Duke University

I have learned throughout my life that what really matters is not whether we have problems but how we go through them.

—**Rosa Parks,** seamstress who sparked the Montgomery, Alabama, bus boycott

Singing is…a way of sharing my spirit in song. I believe the songs in our lives nourish our souls in hard times and elevate them in good times.

—**Gladys Knight,** singer

You must not measure a man by the heights he has reached, but by the depths from which he has come.

—**Frederick Douglass,** (1818–1895), abolitionist and orator

People couldn't understand why my mama would have this blind kid out doing things like cutting wood for the fire. But she had the foresight to go against the grain....Her thing was: "He may be blind, but he ain't stupid."

—**Ray Charles,** musician and singer

I don't *want* to be a role model...because it's a hard task and I'm human. I make mistakes. I'm not perfect. But I will accept the role and I will do it because it's important.

—**Tiger Woods,** golfer

Mistakes are a fact of life. It is the response to the error that counts.

—**Nikki Giovanni,** poet and author

I've always been one to look at a negative and turn it into my favor.

—**Michael Jordan,** businessman and former basketball player, Chicago
Bulls

It doesn't matter how many times you fall down. What matters is how many times you get up.

—**Marian Wright Edelman,** founder and president, Children's
Defense Fund

Do not look where you fell, but where you slipped.

—**African proverb**

You can see that there is no easy walk to freedom anywhere, and many of us will have to pass through the valley of the shadow of death again and again before we reach the mountaintops of our desires.

—**Nelson Mandela,** former president of South Africa

It matters less what you acquire than what you endure to acquire it.

—**Buck O'Neil,** former Negro League baseball player

Opportunity follows struggle. It follows effort. It follows hard work. It doesn't come before.

—**Shelby Steele,** educator and author

We've come a long way, but we've still got a long, long way to go. If you can't run, walk. If you can't walk, crawl. But by all means, keep moving.

—**Martin Luther King Jr.** (1929–1968), civil rights leader and
   Nobel laureate

If one is continually surviving the worst that life can bring, one eventually ceases to be controlled by a fear of what life can bring.

—**James Baldwin** (1924–1987), author

Success is to be measured not so much by the position that one has reached in life as by the obstacles which he has overcome while trying to succeed.

—**Booker T. Washington** (1856–1915), founder, Tuskegee Institute

Stretch Your **Wings**

If there's something you want out of life, you have to go after it. Can't nobody stop you except yourself.

— **Kobe Bryant**

My mother once told me to stay humble, keep a smile on my face and watch how far I can go.

—**Teddy Riley,** singer-songwriter and producer

When you stop a man from dreaming, he becomes a slave.

—**The Artist Formerly Known As Prince,** singer-songwriter and musician

I don't know what the future holds, but I do know who holds the future.

—**Oprah Winfrey,** host and owner, the *Oprah Winfrey Show*

I remember where I came from and I keep that in mind.... If a young female sees the environment I grew up in and sees my dreams and goals come true, [she] will realize [her] dreams and goals might also come true.

—**Jackie Joyner-Kersee,** Olympic gold medalist

It is where you are headed not where you are from that will determine where you end up.

—**Marian Wright Edelman,** founder and president, Children's
Defense Fund

A man's deeds are of greater importance than the facts of his birth.

—**Maasai proverb**

As you grow older, your life must be summed up by more than what you did athletically.

—**Sidney Moncrief,** businessman and former basketball player

We are not powerless in the struggle to determine our fate.

—**Earl G. Graves,** founder, *Black Enterprise* magazine

Only as far as I see can I go, only as much as I dream can I be, only as high as I reach can I grasp.

—**Marva Collins,** founder and director, Westside Preparatory School, Chicago

Never have young people, especially young African Americans, had more opportunities.

—**L. Douglas Wilder,** former governor of Virginia

When you look at the movies, you have to understand that [African Americans] don't just have to act or do makeup. We can direct. We can write. We can be cinematographers. We are a very visual people.

—**Mario Van Peebles,** actor and director

The chances and the opportunities are as wide as this world.

—**John H. Johnson,** founder and CEO, Johnson Publishing Company

I'm just grateful that I'm able to do what I love best, make films. A lot of people spend their entire lives doing a job they hate.
—**Spike Lee,** filmmaker

What you love doing is what you were put here to do.
—**Susan L. Taylor,** editor-in-chief, *Essence* magazine

If you believe you have power, that gives you power, and if you use it, act on it, you can make things happen.
—**Maxine Waters,** U.S. congresswoman

Age is…getting to know all the ways the world turns, so that if you cannot turn the world the way you want, you can at least get out of the way so you won't get run over.
—**Miriam Makeba,** South African singer and political activist

I had a very turbulent life. I had a good life as well, but it was tough....Life does get better. It gets easier as you get older. It really does. Life gets better.

—**Chaka Khan,** singer

Only when you have crossed the river can you say the crocodile has a lump on his snout.

—**Ashanti proverb**

You can do anything you want to do if you want to do it bad enough.

—**Bill Russell,** former basketball player, Boston Celtics

It is my hope that the youth of America will be the antidote to moral pollution and will bring this nation back to its senses.

—**Dick Gregory,** comedian and activist

Our children must never lose their zeal for building a better world. They must not be discouraged from aspiring toward greatness for they are to be the leaders of tomorrow.

—**Mary McLeod Bethune** (1875–1955), president, Bethune-Cookman College

You can't tell the children there's no hope.

—**James Baldwin** (1924–1987), author

The forward pace of the world which you are pushing will be painfully slow. But what of that: the difference between a hundred and a thousand years is less than you now think. But doing what must be done, that is eternal even when it walks with poverty.

—**W. E. B. DuBois** (1868–1963), author and a founder of the NAACP

It is a need of the spirit not to forget whoever has let you feel beautiful and safe. But the past is not the next amazing possibility.
—**June Jordan,** poet and author

I'm not worried about anything from the past. Clearing the inside is what makes dreams come true.
—**Tina Turner,** singer

If you can somehow think and dream of success in small steps, every time you make a step, every time you accomplish a small goal, it gives you confidence to go on from there.
—**John H. Johnson,** founder and CEO, Johnson Publishing Company

I have never felt hopeless or like a victim. I have come to believe that until one learns to love and respect oneself, one will not be able to control one's life and destiny.
—**Maxine Waters,** U.S. congresswoman

We don't have an eternity to realize our dreams, only the time we are here.

—**Susan L. Taylor,** editor-in-chief, *Essence* magazine

You cannot live as though you have a thousand years to accomplish your goals.... It is necessary that you follow your dream *today*.

—**Les Brown,** motivational speaker and author

Is today now?

—**Michael Langworthy,** age 4, Chicago

We mistake our experiences—particularly bad experiences— for indications of who we are and what we deserve. Even when we know we deserve better, we mistake our experiences for the obstacles that can keep us from experiencing more.

—**Iyanla Vanzant,** author and inspirational speaker

Some people judge the present and cancel out the future on the basis of their negative assessment of the past.

—**Jeremiah Wright,** pastor, Trinity United Church of Christ, Chicago

We have come too far to be discouraged or to lose hope or to stop believing in the dream.

—**Coretta Scott King,** founder, the Martin Luther King, Jr. Center for Nonviolent Social Change

I hope that I'll be able to keep seeing "the light," and marching in accordance with it. You can't stop growing—I'm growing now.

—**Gwendolyn Brooks,** poet laureate, Illinois

You must set goals; you must think about how the future will turn out for those who dare to dream.... The tools to use to accomplish...goals are the three "Ps"—Preparation, Patience and Perseverance....Success does not happen overnight.

—**Roland W. Burris,** former comptroller, Illinois

Everything doesn't always happen for the best; but you should make the best out of everything that happens.

—**Berry Gordy,** founder, Motown Industries

Your world is as big as you make it.
I know, for I used to abide
In the narrowest nest in a corner,
My wings pressing close to my side.

—**Georgia Douglas Johnson** (1886–1966), poet and educator

Whether or not you reach your goals in life depends entirely on how well you prepare for them and how badly you want them....You're eagles! Stretch your wings and fly to the sky!

—**Ronald McNair** (1950–1986), astronaut

Index and Biographies

A

Hank Aaron is a retired professional baseball player whose 755 home runs eclipsed the forty-year-old record of Babe Ruth. He serves as a senior vice president and member of the board of directors of the Atlanta Braves. 19, 131

African proverb. 136

Akan proverb. The Akan people comprise several ethnic groups in southern Ghana and the southeast Ivory Coast, West Africa. 106

Muhammad Ali won an Olympic gold medal in boxing in 1960 at the age of eighteen and was the world heavyweight boxing champion an unprecedented three times. 129

Debbie Allen is a choreographer, dancer, actress, producer, and director. She produced and directed the television show *A Different World* and produced the movie *Amistad*. She has frequently choreographed the Academy Awards. 132

Wally "Famous" Amos was the first person to establish stores devoted solely to selling cookies. He is also the author with Stu Gluberman of *Watermelon Magic*. 9

Marian Anderson (1902–1993), considered one of the greatest contraltos of the century, was the first African-American soloist to sing at New York's Metropolitan Opera. 118

Maya Angelou is the author of *I Know Why the Caged Bird Sings, And Still I Rise,* and several other books. She wrote the poem "On the Pulse of Morning" for President Clinton's 1993 inauguration and directed the film *Down in the Delta.* 11, 38, 40, 73, 87, 88, 130

Kofi Annan, United Nations secretary-general, is from Ghana, West Africa. He attended college in Ghana and the United States and has worked for the U.N. for more than thirty years. 41

Louis Armstrong (1901–1971) was an award-winning, innovative trumpet player who also represented the U.S. abroad as an Ambassador of Goodwill. 116

The Artist Formerly Known As Prince (Prince Rogers Nelson) has released more than twenty albums and sold more than 100 million records around the world. He won an Academy Award for Best Film Score for *Purple Rain* in 1983. 68, 140

Molefi Kete Asante is founder and former chairperson of the African American Studies department at Temple University in Philadelphia. 6

Ashanti proverb. The Ashanti people live primarily in Ghana, West Africa. 144

Arthur Ashe (1943–1993) was a champion tennis player and the first black player named to the American Davis Cup team. He wrote a four-volume history of black athletes, *A Hard Road to Glory.* 78

Maurice Ashley, a chess grandmaster, is the coach of two Harlem chess teams, the Raging Rooks and the Dark Knights, perennial winners of the National Junior High School Championship. He is the author of *Maurice Ashley Teaches Chess for Beginning and Intermediate Players,* a multimedia interactive teaching program. 104

B

Erykah Badu (Erica Wright) is a singer and businesswoman; her first album, *Baduism,* which included the number one hit single "On and On," went platinum. In 1997 she contributed to the soundtrack for the film *Eve's Bayou.* 66

Pearl Bailey (1918–1990) had a long career as a dancer, singer, and actress, appearing in several films, including *Carmen Jones*, *St. Louis Blues*, and *Porgy and Bess*. She was also the author of *The Raw Pearl*, *Hurry Up America and Spit*, and other books. 89

James Baldwin (1924–1987), one of this century's finest essayists, also wrote short stories, plays, and novels. His books include *Go Tell It on the Mountain*, *Another Country*, *Nobody Knows My Name*, and *The Fire Next Time*. 17, 89, 106, 137, 145

Tyra Banks is a supermodel and the author of *Tyra's Beauty Inside and Out*. 39, 43, 47

Charles Barkley is an all-star member of the Houston Rockets basketball team. 20

Angela Bassett starred in *Waiting to Exhale* and portrayed Betty Shabazz in *Malcolm X* and Tina Turner in *What's Love Got to Do With It*. 73, 115

Kathleen Battle is an internationally renowned opera singer. 118

Romare Bearden (1912–1988) was an acclaimed artist known for his paintings and collages. He was also a scholar and the author of *Six Black Masters in American Art* and *A History of African American Artists*. 119

W. Kamau Bell is a stand-up comedian. 87

Halle Berry is an actress known for her roles in the movies *Jungle Fever*, *Boomerang*, *Strictly Business*, and *The Last Boy Scout*. She also starred in the television miniseries *Queen* and *The Wedding*. 5, 18, 59

Mary McLeod Bethune (1875–1955) founded a women's school in Daytona Beach, Florida, which in 1923 merged with a men's college to become Bethune-Cookman College. Bethune served as president for many years. 4, 145

Julia A. Boyd is a psychotherapist and the author of *In the Company of My Sisters* and other books. 7, 40, 133

Brandy (Norwood) stars in the television sitcom *Moesha* and is a popular singer and actress whose first album, *Brandy*, went triple platinum. In 1997 she received an NAACP Image Award. 28, 38

Toni Braxton began singing in the church choir at an early age. Her self-titled debut album sold 9.5 million copies and earned her three Grammy Awards, three American Music Awards, and two Soul Train Awards. 130

Gwendolyn Brooks is the author of several books of poetry, including *Winnie*, *To Disembark*, *In the Mecca*, and *Annie Allen*, for which she received a Pulitzer Prize in 1950. She is poet laureate of Illinois and served as poetry consultant to the Library of Congress. 32, 50, 110, 148

Les Brown is a nationally known inspirational speaker and the author of *Live Your Dreams* and *It's Not Over Until You Win*. 16, 147

Kobe Bryant is the youngest member of the Los Angeles Lakers basketball team and an all-star. 114, 139

Roland W. Burris, the first black to win a statewide election in Illinois, has served as state comptroller and attorney general. 149

C

Herman Cain is CEO of Godfather Pizza, president of the National Restaurant Association, and a supporter of the Edmonson Foundation Youth Outreach Program for troubled teens. 122

Bebe Moore Campbell is the author of *Sweet Summer: Growing Up With and Without My Dad, Your*

Blues Ain't Like Mine, Brothers and Sisters, and other books. 47, 78, 87, 88, 99

Pat Campbell works as a diversity marketing strategic planner for Mobil Oil Corporation and is a former Air Force pilot. 97

Tevin Campbell began singing at the age of four and was fifteen when he recorded the multiplatinum album *I'm Ready,* which included the smash hit "Can We Talk." 14

Mariah Carey is a singer and songwriter. She has recorded seven consecutive triple-platinum albums and won Grammy Awards for best new artist and best pop vocal performance by a female. Her albums include *Emotions* and *Daydream.* 4, 10, 127

Benjamin S. Carson is a pediatric neurosurgeon at Johns Hopkins University Hospital in Baltimore. He is also the author of *Gifted Hands* and *Think BIG.* 36, 42, 104, 111

Stephen L. Carter is a professor of law at Yale University and the author of *Reflections of an Affirmative Action Baby.* He clerked for Supreme Court Justice Thurgood Marshall. 109

George Washington Carver (1864–1943), the "Wizard of Tuskegee," was the director of agricultural research at Tuskegee Institute, in Alabama. His discovery of multiple uses for peanuts and sweet potatoes revolutionized southern farming. 70, 84, 108

Ray Charles is a legendary musician and singer who lost his sight at the age of six. His hits include "Georgia on My Mind," "Hit the Road, Jack," "What'd I Say," and "I Can't Stop Loving You." 26, 135

Farai Chideya, a reporter for ABC News, is former national affairs editor for *Vibe* magazine. She is the author of *Don't Believe the Hype: Fighting Cultural Misinformation about African Americans.* 83

Alice Childress is a playwright and novelist. Her works include *A Hero Ain't Nothing but a Sandwich* and *Wedding Band.* 78

Shirley Chisholm became the first African-American female elected to the U.S. House of Representatives in 1964. She is the author of *Unbought and Unbossed.* 67, 89

Pearl Cleage is the author of the novel *What Looks Like Crazy on an Ordinary Day* and the play *Blues for an Alabama Sky* as well as several other works. 58

Eldridge Cleaver (1936–1998) served as minister of information for the Black Panther Party and wrote *Soul on Ice,* a collection of essays. 80

Alice Coachman was the first black woman to win an Olympic gold medal in track and field. She has been inducted into eight halls of fame, including the National Track and Field Hall of Fame. 133

Johnnie Cochran is host of *Cochran & Company* on CNN. He served as lead defense counsel for the O.J. Simpson murder trial and is the author of *Journey to Justice.* Cochran received the first Advocate for Justice Award from the Olender Foundation. 34, 107

Johnnetta B. Cole has served as president of Spelman College and as a member of President Clinton's 1992 transition team. 79

Natalie Cole is a Grammy Award–winning singer whose hit recordings include "Inseparable," "I Live for Your Love," "Our Love," and "Unforgettable." Her father was the legendary jazz and pop singer Nat King Cole. 37, 126

Marva Collins is the founder and director of the renowned Westside Preparatory School in Chicago, and the author of *Marva Collins' Way, Values: Lighting the Candle of Excellence* and other books. 70, 132, 142

Sean "Puffy" Combs is a rapper and producer whose hits include "I'll Be Missing You" and "It's All About the Benjamins." Combs established his own record label, Bad Boy Records, which earned approximately $150 million in 1997. 16, 93, 98, 116

Coolio (Artis Ivey Jr.) is a rap musician whose first solo album was *It Takes a Thief*. He also wrote "Gangsta's Paradise" for the soundtrack of the film *Dangerous Minds*. 56

Bill Cosby is a stand-up comedian, television actor, and the author of *Fatherhood, Time Flies, The Wit and Wisdom of Fat Albert*, and other books. 91

Camille Cosby is a philanthropist and entrepreneur; she is married to comedian and actor Bill Cosby. 99, 107

D-E

Miles Davis (1926–1991) was an innovative and award-winning trumpet player and composer. His albums include *Amandla, Birth of the Cool, Sketches of Spain*, and *Tutu*. 103, 109, 127

Sammy Davis Jr. (1925–1990) was an award-winning singer, dancer, and actor who appeared in films, plays, and on television. He was often called "Mr. Entertainment." 9

Kimberly Dear is a sixteen-year-old writer from Jacksonville, Florida. 21

Frederick Douglass (1818–1895) was enslaved until age twenty but escaped and started *The North Star*, a newspaper devoted to the abolition of slavery. He became a famous orator and an adviser to President Abraham Lincoln. 42, 84, 131, 135

W. E. B. DuBois (1868–1963) was a founder of the NAACP, a professor of history, and the author of more than thirty books, including *The Souls of Black Folk*. 28, 97, 122, 145

Joe Dumars was an all-star member of the Detroit Pistons basketball team. He played on two championship teams and was named Most Valuable Player of the 1989 championship series. 27

Alexandre Dumas, père (1802–1870) was a popular French novelist and playwright whose works include *The Three Musketeers* and *The Man in the Iron Mask*. 106

Tony Dungy is the head coach of the Tampa Bay Buccaneers, one of three African-American head coaches in the NFL. 80

Ed Dwight is an acclaimed bronze sculptor who created a memorial to African Americans who fought in the Revolutionary War for installation in Washington, D.C. 121

Marian Wright Edelman is the founder and president of the Children's Defense Fund, a Washington, D.C., group that lobbies for health, welfare, and justice for children and their families. She is also the author of several books including *Measure of Our Success: A Letter to My Children and Yours* and *Guide My Feet: Prayers and Meditations on Loving and Working For Children*. 49, 122, 136, 141

Kenneth "Babyface" Edmonds, a dominant force in popular music, has written, produced, or performed 111 Top Ten popular songs, including sixteen number one singles. At one time, he had twelve songs on the *Billboard* pop and R&B charts at the same time. 45

Joycelyn Elders, former U.S. surgeon general, is now a professor at the University of Arkansas Medical Science Center, Arkansas Children's Hospital. 48

Mario Elie is a member of the San Antonio Spurs and

a former member of the two-time champion Houston Rockets basketball team. 69

Duke Ellington (1899–1974) was a legendary jazz musician, composer, and bandleader. Some of his most popular compositions are "Mood Indigo," "I Got It Bad and That Ain't Good," and "Sophisticated Lady." 133

Missy Elliott owns The Gold Mind, Inc., a music production company whose debut album, *Supa Dupa Fly,* went platinum. She has also produced, written, and arranged hit songs for Jodeci and Mariah Carey. 103

Ralph Ellison (1914–1994) is the acclaimed author of *Invisible Man,* which won the National Book Award for Fiction in 1953. 9

Ethiopian proverb. Ethiopia is a country in northeastern Africa. 38

Charles Evers is president of the Medgar Evers Fund and the author of *Have No Fear.* He returned to Mississippi after his activist brother, Medgar, was assassinated, in 1963. He served as mayor of Fayette, Mississippi, from 1969 to 1989. 49, 68

Medgar Evers (1925–1963) was a civil rights leader who served as field secretary of the Mississippi Chapter of the NAACP. He was assassinated in 1963. 72

F

Louis Farrakhan is the leader of the Nation of Islam and led the 1995 Million Man March and Day of Atonement in Washington, D.C. 19

Roberta Fields is an educator and school counselor in Chicago. 57

Laurence Fishburne is an actor who was nominated for an Academy Award for his portrayal of Ike Turner in the film *What's Love Got to Do With It.* His other movie credits include *Deep Cover, Othello, Hoodlum,* and *Boyz N the Hood.* 118

George Foreman is a minister, youth leader, and former heavyweight boxing champion of the world. 43, 68

Vivica A. Fox is an actress who appeared in the movies *Independence Day, Soul Food,* and *Set It Off.* She also starred in the television sitcom *Getting Personal.* 48

Aretha Franklin is the multiple-award-winning "Queen of Soul" whose legendary career as a rhythm-and-blues singer has included the hit singles "Respect," "I Never Loved a Man (the Way I Loved You)," and "Freeway of Love." 115

John Hope Franklin is a professor emeritus of history at Duke University. He serves as chairperson of President Clinton's advisory commission on race and is the author of several books, including *From Slavery to Freedom.* 79, 134

Kirk Franklin's youth was plagued with trouble, including drugs and gang violence, but he is now an award-winning gospel artist. His hit recordings include "Watcha Lookin 4," "The Reason Why We Sing," "Silver and Gold," and "Melodies from Heaven." 88

Morgan Freeman is an accomplished actor who is known for his roles in *Driving Miss Daisy, Seven, Glory,* and *The Shawshank Redemption.* 29, 87

Fulani proverb. The Fulani people live in West Africa. 54

S. B. Fuller (1905–1988) was a pioneer in door-to-door sales. He built a conglomerate of companies with sales of more than ten million dollars a year. 18

G

Patrice Gaines overcame a number of personal difficulties to become a reporter for the *Washington Post*. She is the author of *Laughing in the Dark*. 7, 67, 71, 111

Andrea Gardiner, at age sixteen, became the first African American to win the U.S. Junior Ladies Figure Skating Championship. She is an honor student with a 3.5 grade point average. 116

Edward G. Gardner, founder with his wife, Bettiann, of Soft Sheen hair care products, has opened Chicago's first family entertainment center, House of Kicks. 127

Kevin Garnett is an all-star member of the Minnesota Timberwolves basketball team. 94

Marcus Garvey (1887–1940) founded the Universal Negro Improvement Association. He was an adamant advocate for the establishment of black-owned businesses. 97

Henry Louis Gates Jr. is chairperson of Afro-American Studies at Harvard University and the author of several books, including *Colored People* and *Thirteen Ways of Looking at a Black Man*. 20, 119

Nikki Giovanni is a poet and author. Her books include *Black Feeling, Black Talk, Spin a Soft Black Song: Poems for Black Children,* and *Racism 101*. She teaches English at Virginia Polytechnic Institute. 6, 135

Danny Glover is an actor whose film credits include the *Lethal Weapon* series, *The Color Purple,* and *Predator 2*. 65

Whoopi Goldberg is a comedian and actress who has starred in numerous movies since her first, *The Color Purple,* in 1985. In 1990 she won an Oscar for her role in *Ghost*. 2, 47, 51

Cuba Gooding Jr. starred in *Boyz N the Hood* and won the 1997 Academy Award for best supporting actor for his role in the hit film *Jerry Maguire*. 115

Berry Gordy is the founder of Motown Industries, which produced albums by many popular recording artists, including Diana Ross and the Supremes, Smokey Robinson, Marvin Gaye, Martha and the Vandellas, and Stevie Wonder. Motown also produced movies. Gordy was inducted into the Rock and Roll Hall of Fame in 1988. He is the author of *To Be Loved: the Music, the Magic, the Memories of Motown*. 31, 57, 121, 149

Earl G. Graves is the chairperson, editor, and publisher of *Black Enterprise* magazine and CEO of Earl G. Graves Enterprises, Ltd. 141

Dick Gregory is a comedian, social activist, and nutrition advocate. 144

Jasmine Guy is a singer, dancer, and actress who is known for her role as Whitley in the television series *A Different World*. Her film credits include *School Daze, Harlem Nights,* and *A Killer Among Us*. 15, 46

H

Alex Haley (1921–1992) is the famed author of *Roots: The Saga of an American Family,* which became a history-making television miniseries in 1977. He also collaborated in the writing of *The Autobiography of Malcolm X*. 107

M.C. Hammer is a popular rap artist. His hit albums include *Please Hammer Don't Hurt 'Em,* which sold more than ten million copies. 33, 57, 86

Michelle McKinney Hammond is a speaker and author whose books include *What to Do Until Love Finds You* and *Secrets of an Irresistible Woman*. 59, 61

LouRedia Hannah is a kindergarten teacher in Tyler, Texas. 52

Marc Hannah is cofounder of California-based Silicon Graphics, which grossed three billion dollars in 1996. 16

Lorraine Hansberry (1930–1965) was a playwright whose acclaimed work *Raisin in the Sun,* the first play by a black woman to be produced on Broadway, won the New York Drama Critics' Circle Award. 21

LaVan Hawkins is the millionaire owner of nineteen Burger King restaurants and the chairperson and CEO of LaVan Urban City Foods. He grew up in a housing project in Chicago. 84

Heavy D (Dwight Myers) was a member of the rap group Heavy D and the Boyz, whose second and third albums went platinum. He was the executive producer on his solo album *Heavy D Waterbed Hev.* 126

Grant Hill is an all-star member of the Detroit Pistons basketball team. 126

Lauryn Hill won four 1999 NAACP Image Awards for her first solo album, *The Miseducation of Lauryn Hill,* including Outstanding Album and Outstanding New Artist. *The Miseducation of Lauryn Hill* was also awarded five Grammys, including one for Album of the Year. She formerly sang with the Fugees. 1, 106

Chamique Holdsclaw was the all-time leading scorer at the University of Tennessee—male or female. She led her Queens, New York, high school to four state basketball titles and her college team to three straight NCAA championships. She now plays for the Washington Mystics WNBA basketball team. 33

Evander Holyfield is a heavyweight boxing champion who earned an estimated $54 million in 1997. 94

Lena Horne is a legendary singer and actress whose movie credits include the film classics *Cabin in the Sky* and *Stormy Weather.* 8, 51

Dianne Houston is a movie director whose first film, a short feature entitled *Tuesday Morning Ride,* was nominated for an Academy Award. She has also written scripts for Danny Glover, Eddie Murphy, and Oprah Winfrey. 70

Whitney Houston is a popular singer who has won numerous awards. Her successful recordings include "Greatest Love of All," "All at Once," and "I Will Always Love You." She is also pursuing an acting career and starred in *Waiting to Exhale* and *The Bodyguard.* 15

Langston Hughes (1902–1967), a leading writer of the Harlem Renaissance, wrote poetry, plays, novels, essays, biography, history, and short stories. His books include *The Ways of White Folks*, *Weary Blues*, and *Fight for Freedom: The Story of the NAACP.* 119, 123

Zora Neale Hurston (1891–1960), an anthropologist and author, was one of the most gifted artists of the Harlem Renaissance. Her books include the novel *Their Eyes Were Watching God* and her autobiography, *Dust Tracks on a Road.* 39

I-J

Iman (Mohamed Abdulmajid) is an internationally known model and actress who appeared in the movies *The Human Factor, Out of Africa, Star Trek VI,* and *No Way Out.* She is originally from Somalia, East Africa. 51, 123

Allen Iverson, a basketball player with the Philadelphia 76ers, was the NBA's 1996 number one draft choice and the 1996–1997 Rookie of the Year. 5

Bo Jackson, now retired, was one of a very few athletes to play on two professional teams—in his case, baseball and football—at the same time. 103, 105

Janet Jackson is a pop singer who has sold more than forty million albums around the world. She won eight *Billboard* awards for her multiplatinum album *Rhythm Nation, 1814*. 46

Jesse Jackson is a special envoy to Africa appointed by President Clinton. Jackson is also the founder of Operation PUSH and the Rainbow Coalition. He was a candidate for the Democratic nomination for president in 1984 and 1988. 4, 10, 40, 108

Jesse Jackson Jr. is a member of the U.S. House of Representatives from Illinois. 17

Samuel Jackson is an actor whose movie credits include *A Time to Kill, The Long Kiss Goodnight, Die Hard with a Vengeance, Losing Isaiah, Jungle Fever, Pulp Fiction,* and *Eve's Bayou*. 4

Sheneska Jackson is the bestselling author of *Li'l Mama's Rules, Caught Up in the Rapture,* and *Blessings.* 60, 61, 62

T. D. Jakes is a nationally known speaker, minister, and author whose books include *Loose That Man and Let Him Go, Water in the Wilderness,* and *Can You Stand to Be Blessed?* 9, 39

Judith Jamison is a dancer and choreographer and the artistic director of the Alvin Ailey American Dance Theater. 21

Woodlyne Jean-Charles, a seventeen-year-old, won a gold medal in science at the NAACP Afro-Academic, Cultural, Technological and Scientific Olympics (ACT-SO) competition. 3

Mae Jemison, the first female African-American NASA astronaut, is the director of the Jemison Institute

for Advancing Technology in Developing Countries. 27, 71, 117, 119

Cedric Jennings was featured on a *Nightline* news report entitled "Cedric's Journey." He grew up in Washington, D.C., and attended a high school that was considered substandard, then went on to graduate from one of the country's most elite institutions, Brown University. He is the subject of the book *A Hope in the Unseen* by Ron Suskind. 104

Earvin "Magic" Johnson is a businessman and a former member of five Los Angeles Lakers championship basketball teams. He is surviving being HIV positive. 84, 130

Georgia Douglas Johnson (1886–1966) was a poet, educator, and writer whose first collection of poetry, *The Heart of a Woman and Other Poems,* was published in 1918. 149

John H. Johnson is the multimillionaire founder and CEO of Johnson Publishing Company, publishers of *Ebony* and *Jet* magazines. He is also the author of *Succeeding Against the Odds.* 48, 74, 111, 142, 146

Michael Johnson became the first athlete to win gold medals in the 200-meter and 400-meter races in the same Olympic games. He is the author of *Slaying the Dragon*. 106

James Earl Jones, who once suffered from stuttering, is a Tony Award–winning actor who is noted for the quality of his voice. He is featured as the voice of the villain Darth Vader in *Star Wars, The Empire Strikes Back,* and *Return of the Jedi.* His voice is also used as King Mufasa in *The Lion King*. 8

Phillip Jones is chairperson and CEO of Intellectual Properties Management, Inc., in Atlanta. 121

Quincy Jones, winner of more than two dozen Grammys, heads QWest Records, which has produced albums for Michael Jackson, Brandy, Ray Charles, Gloria Estefan, Herbie Hancock, and many others. He has also produced and scored movies and the Academy Awards. 24, 95

June Jordan is a poet, novelist, and essayist. She is the author of *The Voice of the Children, Who Look at Me, Some Changes, His Own Where,* and other books. 146

Michael Jordan is a former member of the six-time NBA champion Chicago Bulls. He has won ten scoring titles, five Most Valuable Player awards for the season, and a Finals Most Valuable Player award for each championship series. He is also a businessman. 24, 56, 76, 117, 125, 136

Florence Griffith Joyner (1959–1998) was known as the world's fastest woman. She won three gold medals at the 1988 Seoul Olympics and still holds world records in the 100- and 200-meter dashes. Joyner, who began running track at age seven, brought style and attention to women's track through her flamboyant outfits and dramatic nails and makeup. 18, 54

Jackie Joyner-Kersee set a record in the heptathlon and won the gold in the long jump at the 1988 Olympic games. She won the heptathlon again in 1992 as well as a bronze medal in the long jump in both 1992 and 1996. 25, 28, 49, 140

K-L

R. (Robert) **Kelly** is a rhythm-and-blues singer and songwriter whose hits include "She's Got That Vibe," "Bump 'N Grind," and "I Believe I Can Fly," which is rapidly becoming a classic. In 1999 he received the Soul Train Sammy Davis Jr. Entertainer of the Year Award. 83

Tracie Kemble serves as vice-president of development for HBO's NYC Productions. 81

Dwayne Kennedy is a stand-up comedian and actor. 82

Kelton "LDB" (Little Drummer Boy) Kessee is a member of the music group Immature. 132

Chaka Khan is an accomplished singer whose recording hits include "I'm Every Woman," "I Feel for You," and "Through the Fire." 144

Dennis Kimbro serves as director of the Clark Atlanta University Center for Entrepreneurship. He is the author of *What Makes the Great, Great* and, with Napoleon Hill, *Think and Grow Rich: A Black Choice.* 67, 73, 74

Coretta Scott King is the widow of Dr. Martin Luther King Jr. and founder of the Martin Luther King, Jr. Center for Nonviolent Social Change in Atlanta. 148

Dexter King, younger son of Coretta Scott King and the late Dr. King, is president of the Martin Luther King, Jr. Center for Nonviolent Social Change. 72

Martin Luther King Jr. (1929–1968) was a civil rights leader who was awarded the 1964 Nobel peace prize. He is also the author of several books, including *Stride Toward Freedom: The Montgomery Story.* 61, 73, 91, 137

Martin Luther King III is a human rights activist and president of the Southern Christian Leadership Conference (SCLC), cofounded by his father, Martin Luther King Jr. 70

Gladys Knight is an award-winning singer, whose hit songs include "I Heard It Through the Grapevine" and "Midnight Train to Georgia." 126, 134

Jawanza Kunjufu is president of the publishing company African American Images and the author of several books, including *Countering the Conspiracy to Destroy Black Boys.* 105

Patti LaBelle won the 1992 Grammy Award for best R&B vocal performance. Her hit songs include "Over the Rainbow," "Lady Marmalade," "New Attitude," and "Somebody Loves You." She received a 1998 *Essence* Award and is the author of *Don't Block the Blessings.* 4, 46, 51, 63, 69, 102

Michael Langworthy lives in Chicago. 147

Queen Latifah is a rap musician and an actress. She starred in the television show *Living Single* and also appeared in the movies *Set It Off, Hoodlum,* and *Sphere.* 14, 66, 85

Jacob Lawrence is an acclaimed artist known for his paintings on the black experience, including the Harriet Tubman series, the Migration series, and the Harlem series. 128

Spike Lee is the CEO of Forty Acres and a Mule Filmworks, Inc., in Brooklyn. He wrote, produced, directed, and acted in *Do the Right Thing, Mo' Better Blues, Get on the Bus, Malcolm X,* and *He Got Game,* among other films. 32, 77, 143

Lisa Leslie is a member of the WNBA Los Angeles Sparks and winner of a gold medal at the 1996 Olympic games. 54

Reginald F. Lewis (1942–1993) was a lawyer, financier, philanthropist, and the CEO of the billion-dollar company TLC Beatrice International Holdings, Inc. 120

Felix H. Liddell is co-editor, with Paula L. Woods, of *I Hear a Symphony: African-Americans Celebrate Love,* as well as other anthologies. 59

LL Cool J (James Todd Smith) is a popular rap musician and actor. His first album, *Radio,* went platinum in 1985 and the single "I Need Love," triple platinum.

He also starred in the television sitcom *In the House* and is the author of *I Make My Own Rules.* 41, 91

Robert Shaw Logan is the owner of Logan Enterprises in Saluda, South Carolina. 99

M

Maasai proverb. The Maasai people live primarily in East Africa. 141

Miriam Makeba is a South African singer and political activist who lived in exile in the United States for many years. She is the author of *Makeba: My Story.* 143

Malcolm X (el-Hajj Malik el-Shabazz) (1925–1965) educated himself in prison, where he joined the Nation of Islam. He founded the Organization for Afro-American Unity and wrote *The Autobiography of Malcolm X,* as well as other books. 6, 37, 41, 74, 101, 107

Malinke proverb. The Malinke people live in West Africa. 19

Karl Malone is the leading scorer for the Utah Jazz basketball team and was named one of the fifty greatest players in the history of the NBA. 53

Nelson Mandela is a social and political activist whose stand against apartheid in South Africa resulted in a twenty-seven-year imprisonment. He was released in 1990 and elected president of South Africa in 1994. 75, 127, 136

Wynton Marsalis is the conductor of the Lincoln Center Jazz Orchestra and the first jazz musician to be awarded a Pulitzer Prize. The acclaimed composer is also considered one of the world's leading classical trumpet virtuosos. He was the recipient of a 1998 *Essence* Award. 69, 112, 123

Thurgood Marshall (1908–1993) was the first black justice appointed to the U.S. Supreme Court. He was the lead attorney for the NAACP from 1938 to 1961. 67

Maxwell is a singer-songwriter, and producer whose debut album, *Maxwell's Urban Hang Suite*, went platinum. 60

Benjamin E. Mays (1895–1984), whose parents had been enslaved, became president of Morehouse College, in Atlanta, where he served from 1940 to 1968. His autobiography is entitled *Born to Rebel*. 50, 118

Nathan McCall is the author of the books *Makes Me Wanna Holler* and *What's Going On* and a writer for the *Washington Post*. 82

Ronald McNair (1950–1986) was a NASA astronaut. He died in the explosion of the space shuttle *Challenger*. 150

Daniel Miller Jr., age ten, is president and CEO of Daniel Miller Jr.'s Custom Postcards in Pittsburgh. He is also a straight-A student and a writer. 96

Sybil Mobley is dean of the business school at Florida A&M University, in Tallahassee. 120

Sidney Moncrief, a former basketball player for the Milwaukee Bucks, is the owner of a car dealership, a father of four, and active in community service. 141

Monica (Arnold) made her first recording at age thirteen and was fourteen when "Don't Take It Personal" and "Before You Walk Out Of My Life" both went platinum. She sang "For You I Will" on the five-million-selling *Space Jam* movie soundtrack. 24, 35, 86, 102

Nathan Morris is a member of the musical group Boyz II Men, whose hit recordings include "End of the Road" and "On Bended Knee." 76

Wanya Morris is a member of the musical group Boyz II Men, whose hit recordings include "End of the Road" and "On Bended Knee." 40, 114

Toni Morrison is the 1993 Nobel Laureate in Literature and the author of *Paradise, Beloved, The Bluest Eye*, and other novels. 13, 63, 90, 102

Carol Moseley-Braun became the first African-American woman elected to the United States Senate in 1992. 15, 77

Walter Mosley is the award-winning author of the Easy Rawlins mysteries: *Gone Fishin', Devil in a Blue Dress, A Red Death, White Butterfly*, and *Black Betty*. His novels have been translated into seventeen languages. 38, 78

Ava Muhammad is an author and an attorney for the Nation of Islam. 58, 62

Eddie Murphy is a comedian, actor, and producer, whose film credits include *Trading Places, Beverly Hills Cop, The Nutty Professor, Coming to America, The Golden Child*, and *Harlem Nights*. 3, 32, 116

N-O

Itabari Njeri is a contributing editor to the *Los Angeles Times Magazine* and author of *Every Good-bye Ain't Gone*, winner of the 1990 American Book Award. 83

Shaquille O'Neal is an all-star member of the Los Angeles Lakers basketball team and the owner of TWISM, a clothing manufacturer in Inglewood, California. 23, 94

John Jordan "Buck" O'Neil Jr. was a player with the Kansas City Monarchs of the Negro National Baseball League and serves as board chairperson of the Negro League Baseball Museum in Kansas City, Missouri. 137

P

Clarence Page is a Pulitzer Prize–winning syndicated columnist for the *Chicago Tribune*. 89

Rosa Parks is a seamstress who refused to give up her seat on a Montgomery, Alabama, bus in 1955 and sparked a movement that ended legalized racial discrimination. She is founder and president of the Rosa and Raymond Parks Institute for Self-Development. 50,134

Jarrett Payton is an outstanding high school athlete. His dad is the Hall of Fame football player Walter Payton. 5

Walter Payton is a businessman, Hall of Fame football player, and former member of the Chicago Bears. 33

Sidney Poitier is an actor, producer, and director. In 1963, he became the first African American to win an Academy Award for best actor, for *Lilies of the Field*. He has starred in numerous films and directed *Uptown Saturday Night, Stir Crazy, Buck and the Preacher,* and *Let's Do It Again.* 62

Colin Powell is chairperson of America's Promise — The Alliance for Youth. A retired U.S. Army general, he was the first African American to chair the Joint Chiefs of Staff. His bestselling autobiography is entitled *My American Journey.* 16, 21, 79, 117, 131

Kevin Powell is a former staff writer for *Vibe* magazine and the author of *Keepin' It Real: Post-MTV Reflections on Race, Sex and Politics.* 88

Richard Pryor is a stand-up comedian, actor, and the author of *Pryor Convictions.* 7, 27, 77, 80

R

Teddy Riley is a producer, songwriter, and singer. He has produced hit songs for many superstars, including Patti LaBelle, Bobby Brown, and Michael Jackson. 140

Paul Robeson (1898–1976) was a renowned concert singer, lawyer, actor, All-American football player, scholar, and political activist. He performed the title role in *Othello* on Broadway and appeared in a number of plays, including *Porgy and Bess* and *Showboat.* Because of his political beliefs he was barred from concert halls in the U.S. and denied a passport so he couldn't earn a living abroad. 31, 79

Sugar Ray Robinson (1921–1989) dominated the middleweight divisions in boxing and won his first world championship in 1950. He was inducted into the International Boxing Hall of Fame in 1990. 17

Chris Rock is a stand-up comedian, actor, and the host of an HBO talk show. 2

Roshumba (Williams) is a fashion model whose hair is short and natural. 52

Diana Ross is the former lead singer of the Supremes. She starred in the movies *Mahogany* and *Lady Sings the Blues* and is the author of *Secrets of a Sparrow.* 31, 114, 129

Wilma Rudolph (1940–1994) overcame the crippling effects of scarlet fever to make history at the 1960 Olympics by becoming the first American woman to win three gold medals in track and field. 37

Bill Russell was a star player of eleven Boston Celtics championship basketball teams and was named one of the fifty greatest players in the history of the NBA. 144

S

John Salley won three NBA championships playing with the Detroit Pistons and the Chicago Bulls. 94

Salt (Cheryl James) is a member of the musical group Salt-N-Pepa. Salt, Pepa, and Spinderella wrote, arranged, and produced their album *Brand New*. They won a Grammy in 1994. 36

Gamilah Shabazz is a daughter of Malcolm X and Betty Shabazz. 30

Ilyasah Shabazz is a daughter of Malcolm X and Betty Shabazz. 29

Millicent Shelton is the writer and director of the movie *Ride*. 81

Sinbad (David Adkins) is a comedian and actor who has starred in movies and who appeared in the television series *A Different World*. He also hosted the television show *Vibe*, and has had his own television specials. 2, 26, 36, 90, 98

John Singleton is a screenwriter and director whose film credits include *Boyz N the Hood, Poetic Justice,* and *Higher Learning*. 41

Maceo Sloan is CEO of Sloan Financial Group, based in Durham, North Carolina. 95

Jada Pinkett Smith is a popular actress known for her roles in the movies *Set It Off, Jason's Lyric, The Nutty Professor, Scream 2,* and *Woo*. She is married to rap musician and actor Will Smith. 37, 53, 55

Will Smith is a rap musician and actor in television and film. He starred in *Independence Day* and *Men in Black* and was the recipient of a 1998 *Essence* Award. Smith received a 1999 Grammy for Best Rap Solo Performance for "Gettin' Jiggy Wit It" from the multi-platinum album *Big Willie Style*. 20, 26, 34, 76, 94

Wesley Snipes is an acclaimed actor whose film credits include *Mo' Better Blues, New Jack City, Jungle Fever, White Men Can't Jump,* and *Down in the Delta*. 30, 46, 82

Shelby Steele is a research fellow at the Hoover Institute at Stanford University and the author of *The Content of Our Character*. 81, 137

Percy Sutton is cofounder and board chairperson of Inner City Broadcasting, in New York City. 120

Keith Sweat is a popular singer and coproducer whose hit recordings include *Make It Last Forever, I Want Her, Make You Sweat,* and *I'll Give All My Love to You*. 60

T-V

Brenda Tapia is the founder and director of the Love of Learning Program at Davidson College, a college-preparatory program for African-American students. 58, 91, 99

Regina Taylor is a playwright and film, television, and stage actress who starred in the movies *Losing Isaiah* and *Clockers* and the television series *I'll Fly Away* and *Children of the Dust*. Her plays include *The Ties That Bind* and *Escape from Paradise*. 96

Susan L. Taylor is editor-in-chief of *Essence* magazine and the author of *In the Spirit, Lessons in Living,* and other books. 39, 52, 96, 143, 147

Michael Thurmond holds degrees in theology and philosophy and is the director of welfare for the state of Georgia. Thurmond's family received welfare from the time he was very young through his junior high school years. 128

Robert Townsend is a stand-up comedian, writer,

director, and actor whose film credits include *Hollywood Shuffle, Meteor Man,* and *The Five Heartbeats.* 25

Tunisian proverb. Tunisia is a country in northern Africa. 17

Tina Turner is a Grammy Award–winning singer whose hit recordings include "What's Love Got to Do With It," "A Fool in Love," and "Proud Mary." 2, 19, 146

Blair Underwood is an actor whose credits include the television shows *The Cosby Show* and *L.A. Law* as well as films, including *Set It Off.* Blair constantly moved as a child because his father was an army sergeant stationed all over the U.S. and in Germany. 128

Usher (Raymond IV) is a singer and actor who plays Brandy's romantic interest on the sitcom *Moesha.* He was nominated for a Grammy Award for his hit recording "You Make Me Wanna." 15

Mario Van Peebles is an actor and director. He directed the films *Posse* and *New Jack City* and coproduced (with his father, Melvin Van Peebles) and directed *Panther.* He also has numerous television credits. 142

Iyanla Vanzant is an inspirational speaker, Yoruba priestess, and the bestselling author of *Acts of Faith, Tapping the Power Within,* and several other books. 42, 60, 147

W-Z

Alice Walker is the award-winning author of several novels, including *The Color Purple, Meridian,* and *The Third Life of Grange Copeland.* She also writes poetry and essays. 42, 92, 133

Madam C. J. Walker (1867–1919) created, developed, and manufactured hair care products. She also built a factory and trained women to sell her products, becoming the first female self-made millionaire in the U.S. 72, 98

Booker T. Washington (1856–1915) was born into slavery but went on to become the founder and first president of Tuskegee Institute in Alabama, and an adviser to U.S. presidents. 54, 96, 109, 138

Denzel Washington won the Oscar for best supporting actor in *Glory* and the New York Film Critics Award for the title role in *Malcolm X.* 30, 56, 66

Maxine Waters served fourteen years in the California State Assembly before being elected to the United States House of Representatives. 8, 143, 146

Rolonda Watts is an entrepreneur who hosted the television show *Rolonda.* 71

Damon Wayans is an award-winning actor, writer, and stand-up comedian. His film credits include *The Last Boy Scout* and *Mo' Money,* for which he was also executive producer. 29

Keenen Ivory Wayans is an award-winning producer, screenwriter, director, and television and film actor. His television credits include *In Living Color* and *The Keenen Ivory Wayans Show.* His film credits include *I'm Gonna Git You Sucka* and *Low Down Dirty Shame.* He is the oldest of the Wayans siblings. 95

Marlon Wayans is costar of the television sitcom *The Wayans Brothers.* He is the younger brother of Damon and Keenen. 90

Alek Wek is an international fashion model. She is a Dinka from Sudan, in northeastern Africa. 53

John Edgar Wideman is an English professor and writer whose books include *Brothers and Keepers,*

Fatheralong, A Glance Away, Sent for You Yesterday, and *Philadelphia Fire.* 34, 86

L. Douglas Wilder became the first African American to be elected a state governor (of Virginia in 1989). 105, 142

Montel Williams is the host of a television talk show and the author of *Mountain, Get Out of My Way.* 129

Vanessa Williams is a singer and star of Broadway and film. Her movie credits include *Soul Food, Hoodlum,* and *Eraser.* In 1996 she received the Lady of Soul Lifetime Achievement Award and in 1998 won an NAACP Image Award. 63

Venus Williams won the Lipton Championship two years in a row and is ranked as one of the top ten women's tennis players in the world. At ages eighteen and seventeen, respectively, she and her sister Serena made history twice in 1999. They both won Women's Tennis Association championships on the same day in March, and later in the month played each other in the title match of the Lipton Championship. The Williams sisters are managed and coached by their father, Richard. 20

Oprah Winfrey hosts the *Oprah Winfrey Show,* the highest-rated TV talk show in history. Winfrey, who founded her own TV production company, Harpo Productions, in 1986, has won numerous awards including nine Emmys, a Lifetime Achievement Award, and several NAACP image awards. She has also acted in numerous films including *The Color Purple* and *Beloved.* Winfrey is considered one of the most recognizable personalities in the United States. 10, 62, 110, 113, 140

Wolof proverb. The Wolof people live in Senegal on the west coast of Africa. 5

Stevie Wonder is a singer, songwriter, and musician who was inducted into the Rock and Roll Hall of Fame in 1989. His hits include "For Once in My Life," "My Cherie Amour," and "You Are the Sunshine of My Life." He lost his sight shortly after his premature birth. 68

Paula L. Woods is co-editor, with Felix H. Liddell, of *I Hear a Symphony: African-Americans Celebrate Love* and other anthologies. 59

Tiger Woods is the golfing sensation who won more than two million dollars in his first year of professional golf, when he was twenty-one years old. 14, 25, 135

Jeremiah Wright is the pastor of Trinity United Church of Christ, in Chicago, and the author of *What Makes You So Strong?* 148

Richard Wright (1908–1960) is the author of *Native Son, Black Boy, Uncle Tom's Children,* and several other books. 80, 110

Yoruba proverb. The Yoruba people live primarily in Nigeria, West Africa. 7, 61

Andrew Young is a former congressman who also served as mayor of Atlanta from 1982 to 1990 and was cochair of the Atlanta Committee for the 1996 Olympic Games. 108

Coleman Young (1918–1997) was called the politics and soul of Detroit. He was mayor from 1974 to 1993. 134

Contacting the Authors

We hope you have enjoyed *Stretch Your Wings: Famous Black Quotations For Teens,* and we would like your feedback. To contact the authors, please use the following,

Janet Cheatham Bell
Lucille Usher Freeman
Stretch Your Wings
P.O. Box 428392
Evergreen Park, IL 60805

HYPERLINK mail to:
belljan@earthlink.net
HYPERLINK mail to:
lfreeman@ameritech.net

The authors are also available for book readings and signings as their schedules permit.

Photographs used by permission of: NASA (p. iv); Reuters/Sam Mircovich/Archive Photos (p. 1); Andrea Renault/Globe Photos, Inc. (p. 13); Miranda Shen/Fotos International/Archive Photos (p. 23); Fotos International/Archive Photos (p. 35); Archive Photos/Lee (p. 45); Victor Malafronte/Archive Photos (p. 55); Michelle Bega, Rogers & Cowen (p. 65); Archive Photos/AMW Pressedienst (p. 75); Reuters/Fred Prouser/Archive Photos (p. 85); John Barrett/Globe Photos, Inc. (p. 93); Express Newspapers/Archive Photos (p. 101); Popperfoto/Archive Photos (p. 113); Joshua Dreyfuss/NBC/Globe Photos (p. 125); Andrew D. Bernstein/ NBA Photos (p. 139).

Excerpts from the following poems are gratefully acknowledged:

"To Young Readers," by Gwendolyn Brooks, from *Very Young Poets,* by Gwendolyn Brooks, copyright © 1991. Published by Third World Press, Chicago. Reprinted by permission of the author. "Hold Fast to Dreams," by Langston Hughes, from *Collected Poems,* by Langston Hughes, copyright © 1994 by the Estate of Langston Hughes, reprinted by permission of Alfred A. Knopf, Inc.; "Your World," by Georgia Douglas Johnson, from *American Negro Poetry,* edited by Arna Bontemps, copyright © 1963, 1974 by Georgia Douglas Johnson, reprinted by permission of Farrar, Straus & Giroux, Inc.